Celts, Flakes and Bifaces –
The Garo Hills Story

SOUTH ASIAN ARCHAEOLOGY SERIES

EDITED BY ALOK K. KANUNGO   No. 7

Celts, Flakes and Bifaces – The Garo Hills Story

Sukanya Sharma

Assistant Professor, Dept. of Humanities and Social Sciences
Indian Institute of Technology Guwahati, Guwahati-781039, INDIA

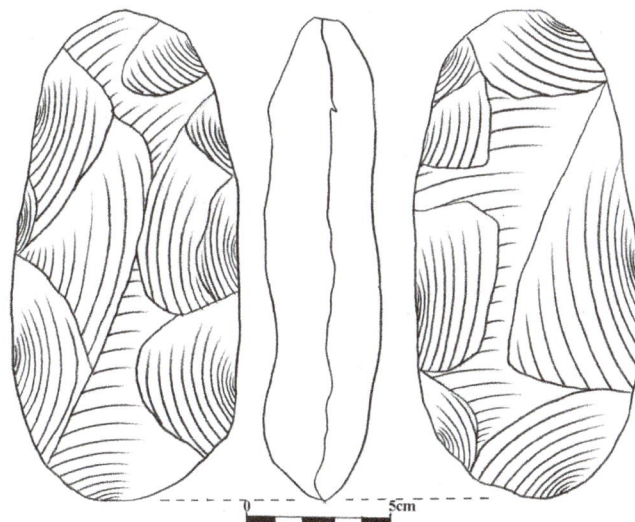

BAR International Series 1664
2007

Published in 2019 by
BAR Publishing, Oxford

BAR International Series 1664

South Asian Archaeological Series No. 7
Series Editor: Alok K. Kanungo

Celts, Flakes and Bifaces – The Garo Hills Story

© S Sharma and the Publisher 2007

ISBN   9781407300689 paperback
ISBN   9781407331386 e-book

DOI   https://doi.org/10.30861/9781407300689

A catalogue record for this book is available from the British Library

This book is available at www.barpublishing.com

BAR Publishing is the trading name of British Archaeological Reports (Oxford) Ltd.
British Archaeological Reports was first incorporated in 1974 to publish the BAR
Series, International and British. In 1992 Hadrian Books Ltd became part of the BAR
group. This volume was originally published by John and Erica Hedges Ltd. in
conjunction with British Archaeological Reports (Oxford) Ltd / Hadrian Books Ltd,
the Series principal publisher, in 2007. This present volume is published by BAR
Publishing, 2019.

BAR
PUBLISHING

BAR titles are available from:

       BAR Publishing
       122 Banbury Rd, Oxford, OX2 7BP, UK
EMAIL info@barpublishing.com
PHONE +44 (0)1865 310431
FAX   +44 (0)1865 316916
       www.barpublishing.com

Foreword

Alok Kumar Kanungo
Series Editor, South Asian Archaeology Series
International Series of British Reports

The International Series of British Archaeological Reports, with its 1500 titles to the present time, is undoubtedly one of the most important places of publication in the discipline of Archaeology. But it is a pity that works on the archaeology of South Asia have been less represented in the series than their interest and value deserves.

The archaeological record of South Asia (comprising India, Pakistan, Nepal, Bhutan, Bangladesh, Sri Lanka and the Maldives) is extremely rich. This wealth begins in the Lower Palaeolithic period and includes, for example, the Harappan Civilization, one of the oldest in the world (covering a very large area and having many unique features -- the most ancient known town planning, its architecture and high standards of civic hygiene, its art, iconography, paleography, numismatics and international trade). South Asia also has a large number of earlier, contemporary, and later Neolithic and Chalcolithic cultures. Moreover, what makes South Asia particularly significant for the study of past human behaviour is the survival of many traditional modes of life, like hunting-gathering, pastoralism, shifting cultivation, fishing, and fowling, the study of which throws valuable light on the reconstruction of past cultures. In the region there are a large number of government and semi-government institutions devoted to archaeological teaching and/or research in archaeology and a large and professionally trained body of researchers.

Of course, a number of universities and other institutions, in the area do have their own publication programmes and there are also reputed private publishing houses. However, British Archaeological Reports, a series of 30 years standing, has an international reputation and distribution system. In order to take advantage of the latter – to bring archaeological researches in South Asia to the notice of scholars in the western academic world – the South Asian Archaeology Series has been instituted within the International Series of British Archaeological Reports. This series (which it is hoped to associate with an institution of organization in the area) aims at publishing original research works of international interest in all branches of archaeology of South Asia.

Those wishing to submit books for inclusion in the South Asian Archaeology Series should contact the South Asian Archaeology Series Editor, who will mediate with John Hedges, one of the BAR Editors and publishers of BAR, in Oxford. The subject has to be appropriate and of the correct academic standard (*curriculum vitae* are requested and books may be referred); instructions for formatting will be given, as necessary.

Dr. Alok Kumar Kanungo
Department of Archaeology
Deccan College Post-Graduate & Research Institute
Pune 411006
INDIA
email: alok_kanungo@yahoo.com

ACKNOWLEDGEMENTS

This book is actually the outcome of my doctoral research which I undertook in Deccan College Post- graduate and Research Institute, Pune-6, from 1997 to 2001, under the guidance of Prof. K Paddayya. His presence as my Supervisor provided me courage to undertake this research project in an archaeologically lesser known area of the country. His emphasis on perfection while writing my thesis titled "Cultural Affinities between Southeast Asia and Northeast India during Prehistoric Times with special reference to Ganol and Rongram Valleys in Meghalaya" made me aware of my short comings which have helped me immensely in writing this book. I sincerely thank him.

Numerous academic discussions with Prof. S.N. Rajguru on geomorphology immensely contributed to my understanding of the landscape of the study area specifically and the region as a whole. I am grateful to him for his constant help and encouragement. I sincerely thank Dr. Sheila Mishra for her invaluable suggestions and observations on the typology of the artifacts and analysis of the sediments and Dr. Richa Jhaldiyal for helping me constantly with constructive suggestions whenever obstructions deterred my path.

A special thanks to Prof. Rasmi Shoocongdej, Late Prof. Surin Pookajorn and Dr. Surapol Natapintu from the Department of Archaeology, Silpakorn University, Bangkok for the valuable academic and non-academic assistance during my two months field work in Thailand. The junior fellowship awarded by the Indian Council of Historical Research provided some respite from the financial hurdles. I am also specially grateful to the Jawaharlal Nehru Memorial Fund for awarding me the scholarship for undertaking field work in Thailand for two months.

Field Work in Garo Hills would not have been possible without the constant help of Agath Sangma, resident of Selbalgiri Village, Garo Hills. Thank you seems to be a small word for the amount I owe to him. He is one of the strongest pillars on which this work stands.

I would like to acknowledge the help and co-operation offered by Mr. H. Kariyanna, Dr. U.V. Mishra and Mr. Kongla of the Geological Survey of India, Shillong in the collection of geological data and also for assisting me in my field work.

I would also like to thank Mr. Julius Marak, Museologist, State Museum, Shillong and Ms. Sahane Marak, Assistant Curator, District Museum, Tura for their co-operation during my field work in Garo Hills.

I thank Dr. A. Kshirsagar, from the Chemistry Laboratory, Deccan College for providing me the facilities for the chemical analysis of the soil samples and Vaishale Kathale for assisting me. I am also grateful to Mr. Sharad Kute, Ms. Trupti More and Ms. Urmila Jagtap from the Deccan College library for aiding me in various ways in my library work.

Love and affection of my dear friends Viraj, Sharmi, Vaishali, Vasundhara, Nilesh, Rhea and Kurush, has provided me immense relief and joy during all these years of my stay in Pune. Expressing my deep feelings of gratitude I would like to say that to them I owe the days of my happiness in Pune. Besides them I am also grateful to numerous other friends in the campus specially Shahida with whom I have shared my joys and sorrows.

Deesha, my daughter and Monojit, my husband are two new additions in my life after completing my doctoral research. Deesha, my guiding angel showed me the path of fulfilment and I traversed on that path to write this book. But it would have never been possible without the encouragement and support of Monojit. My parents have been a great source of inspiration. I thank them all.

CONTENTS

LIST OF FIGURES

LIST OF PLATES

x

INTRODUCTION

The prehistoric lithic assemblage of Northeast India is distinctive in character. It is a synthesis of two types of cultural traits, Southeast Asian and Indian. Artifacts with Southeast Asian cultural traits are shouldered celts, short axes and chord marked pottery and the Indian cultural traits are the bifaces (Plates 1 & 2).

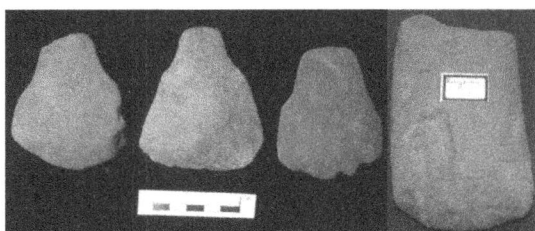

Plate 1: Celts

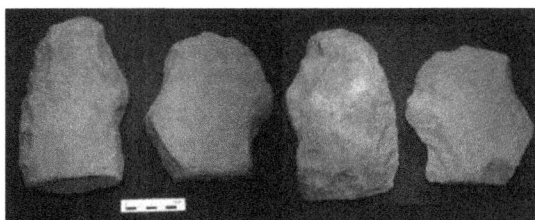

Plate 2: Biface

The ground and polished celts found abundantly and the chord marked sherds were the only type of convincing evidence of the prehistoric period from this area. The amorphous flakes and flake blades present abundantly were relegated to the position of being debitage of the celt manufacturing process ignoring their stratigraphic position, as retouching was absent or minimum and the shapes amorphous. Pebble tools were reported from the area since 1974. But the claims of the scholars from the region that they belong to the Palaeolithic chopper-chopping tradition were not convincing. The reasons behind this are that the typology of these tools did not match their Indian counterparts and the geology of the region was different for which the stratigraphy was not clear. For giving meaning to the archaeological record of the region a holistic approach was necessary for understanding the regional geomorphology, the post-depositional processes distinctive to the region together with the typology and technology of the tools.

Objective

Through this work a regional archaeological structure was developed. Initiated by ecological considerations this model was adopted to understand the adaptability conditions developed by the prehistoric inhabitants of the area. Situated between two different environmental systems the monsoonal tropics and the tropical rainforest zone the regional ecology of Northeast India have had a major role in the growth and development of human culture in the area. Affinities between the Neolithic tools of Southeast Asia and Northeast India were very clear. But certain bifacial artifacts are also similar to certain middle Palaeolithic assemblages from other parts of India. These are adaptability conditions indigenous to the region. This explains the relationship between prehistoric human behaviour and observable archaeological record of the region.

It has been stated that due to several factors the archaeological record is spatially continuous and its structure may be described in terms of variable artifact density across a landscape. This is what is referred to as regional archaeological structure and 'off-site' approach is designed to utilize the spatial continuity to maximize archaeological information (Foley 1981: 2). The lithic artifacts, the alluvial mounds or deposits within which the artifacts are found and the present lifestyle of the inhabitants of the area are the only type of data available in the study area for reconstructing the life ways of the prehistoric people. The data looks insufficient but the man-land relationship in the area has produced this data. Interpreting this man-land relationship in the light of the present theoretical developments in the discipline will bring us closer to the truth.

The Study Area

For this study the Ganol and Rongram river valleys in Garo Hills, Meghalaya was chosen on the basis of its potentialities in terms of archaeological sites. The archaeological record of prehistoric man reported from the area seems to be extremely rich. A wide variety of tools typologically representing almost all periods of prehistory are present in the lithic assemblage of Garo hills. The pebble tools with Hoabinhian affinities were first reported from this area. Earlier workers have reported a variety of flake tools and bifaces.

Methodology

A reconnaissance survey of the Ganol and Rongram river basins was made with the help of topographic maps of the area prepared by the Survey of India. The upper and middle stretches of the courses of both the rivers were chosen for study. The confluence of both the rivers marked the last point of the study area.

A drainage map (Fig. 1) of the study area was prepared on which surface scatters of artifacts were plotted. Then, through a systematic survey involving walking across the landscape, localities were identified, as the 'sites' or 'off-sites' were classified. Areas with low artifact density were marked as 'off-site' or 'non-site' areas.

Data collection was done through stratified random sampling method. As required in the method the area was divided into two natural zones; cultivated land and non-cultivated land. Almost 70% of the area is cultivated land and accordingly 70% of squares or grids were made on cultivated land. Sampling was done with appropriate grid numbers. Trial trenching and section scraping were done at a few selected places. Ethno-archaeological data was collected by adopting the methods of scientific field observation and interview method.

The method of observation was used in the study of collective behaviour and complex social situations of the Garos, who are local inhabitants of the area under study. Scientists used methods of non-controlled and controlled observation for collecting data. In this work non-controlled participant method was adopted. In non-controlled observation careful scrutiny of real life situation was made without the use of instruments of precision. As a participant observer I lived with Garo families and observed their lifestyle with special emphasis on subsistence pattern.

The interview method was used to collect data on specific topics like house type, land use pattern, traditional soil conservation techniques and food habits. Interview can be defined as an instrument of research and discovery through the process of skilled interrogation. A set of questions was formulated with the help of which a cross-section of people of the Garo society was interviewed.

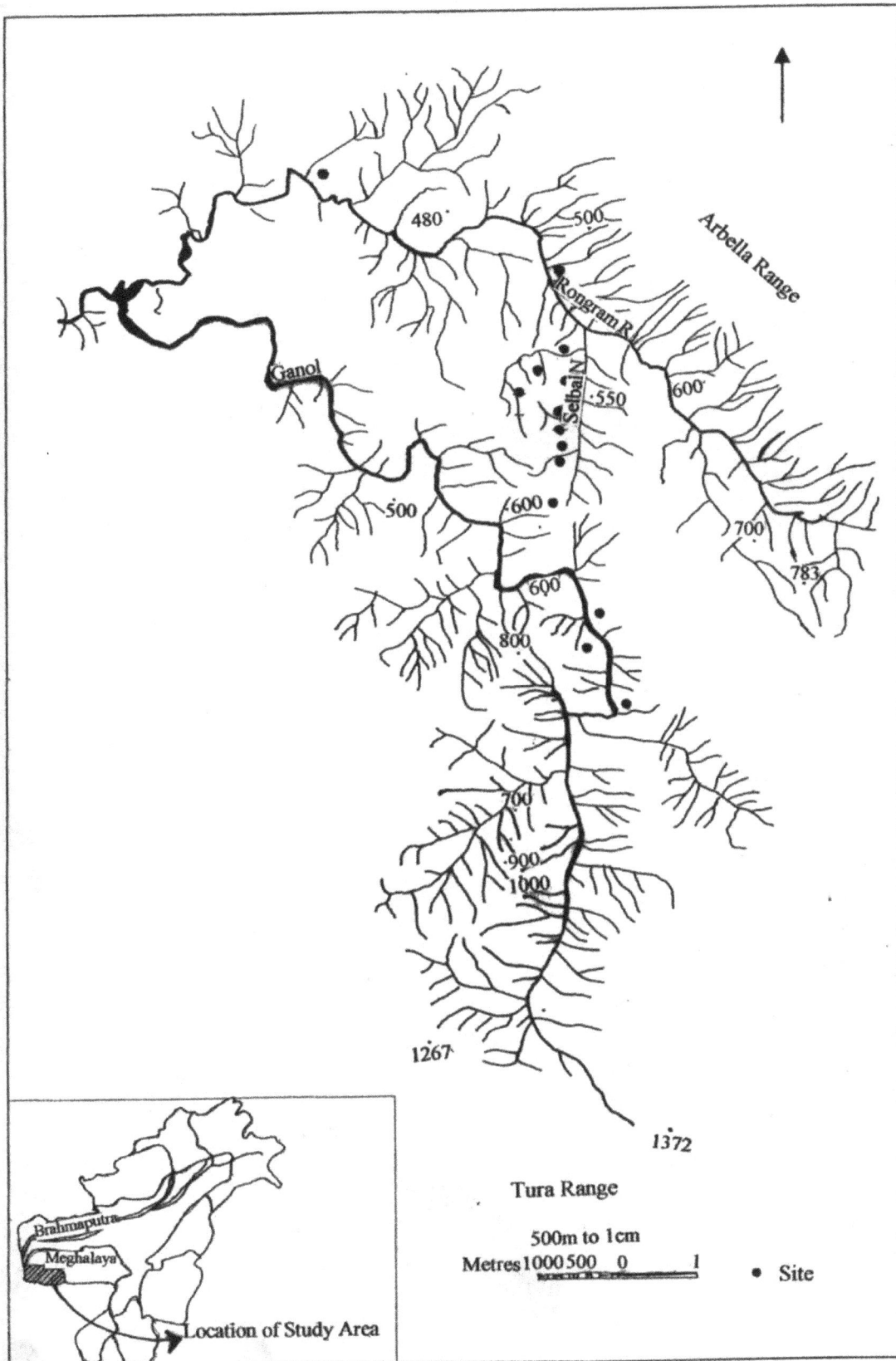

Figure 1: Drainage Map of Ganol and Rongram River Valleys

LATE PLEISTOCENE AND EARLY HOLOCENE IN INDIA AND SOUTHEAST ASIA

Late/Terminal Pleistocene and Early Holocene Cultures of India

The Late/Terminal Pleistocene cultures of India include the Upper Palaeolithic and a part of the Mesolithic cultures while the early Holocene cultures include a part of the Mesolithic and the whole of Neolithic. These cultures in absolute years have been dated between 40,000 yrs and 1,500 yrs B.P.

The changes in stone tools and in methods of making them which characterize the Upper Palaeolithic coincide with the last phases of the Pleistocene, when the last glaciation was coming to an end and sea levels were rising (Allchin and Allchin 1997: 71, 72, 74). The Indian Upper Palaeolithic can be divided into three major techno-typological groupings:

(1) Flake-blade industries

(2) Blade-tool industries and

(3) Blade and burin industries.

The flake-blade industries are characterised by relatively broad blades suggesting a crude stage of blade tool technology. Scrapers, points, and borers made mostly on flakes and flake-blades are the common types, but scrapers form the predominant element. This assemblage is better known from the Singbhum district in Bihar.

The blade-tool industries constitute large to small sized blades, backed blade tools and scrapers, points, awls and burins on flakes, flake-blade and blades. The important feature of the blade tool industry is the regularisation of the blade-tool technology. This industry has been reported from several open air riverine sites in the states of Karnataka, Maharashtra, Uttar Pradesh, Andhra Pradesh and Madhya Pradesh.

The distinctive feature of the blade and burin industry is the predominant blade, backed blade and burin element. The evidence recorded from the primary open air riverine

sites around Renigunta is the best known in this group. It forms a distinct technological entity on the Southeastern coast of India (Murty 1979: 303-305).

Further to the north in the Belan and Son valleys Upper Palaeolithic artifacts are associated with gravels at the beginning of the third cycle of deposition, while in the Belan sequence they are dated by C^{14} between *c.* 25,000 and *c.* 19,000 yrs. ago and in the Son sequence to *c.* 10,000 yrs. ago. Chopani Mando in the Belan valley, excavated in the 1970's showed a sequence of occupation from Upper Palaeolithic to Neolithic. The range of artifacts is similar to those described from the Upper Palaeolithic of Pushkar in Rajasthan. Parallel sided blades, small blade cores and flakes and a few geometric microliths are the common tool types. Animal bones were found throughout the excavation at Chopani Mando and fossil bones identified in the gravels of all four depositional cycles of the Belan river suggest that then sheep and goats were successfully domesticated (Allchin and Allchin 1997: 79) The excavation at Patne in Maharashtra showed that the Upper Palaeolithic inhabitants of the area began consuming wild food grains. Bone tools of the period have been reported from Billa Surgam caves in the Kurnool area of Andhra Pradesh excavated by Robert Bruce Foote in 1885 and Muchchatla Chintamani Gavu cave in the same area excavated by M.L.K. Murty.

The stone industry during the Pleistocene/Holocene transition was microlithic. Very convincing evidence of microlithic assemblages of the period have come from the Tarafeni valley of West Bengal and upland western Maharashtra. Occurrence of several vertebrate fossils on the surface of calcrete at Dhuliapur in the Tarafeni Valley indicates late Pleistocene age of the artifact-bearing colluvial deposits. The formation of pedogenic calcrete in a sub-humid environment with an average annual rainfall of 1600-2000 mm, suggests the presence of semi-aridity in late/terminal

Pleistocene period (Basak *et al.* 1998: 731). A review of available radiocarbon dates from different sites of the Pravara river basin like Nevasa, Inamgaon, Chandri, Kalas Asla etc. show that the gravel units within the late Pleistocene alluvium belong to arid phases of this period. At both Nevasa and Sangama gravels with microliths date to 12.8 kyr. At Nevasa a second gravel with blade tools dates to 16.4 kyr, while at Inamgaon there were two dates of 19 kyr and 21 kyr for gravel with Upper Palaeolithic blade tools. This aggradational episode might be correlated to the last glacial maximum. Some gravel units associated with blade tools date to 25 kyr and probably belong to an earlier arid phase younger than 40 kyr. (Sadakata *et al.* 1995: 43, 44, 53). Thus, in the Pravara river basin of Maharashtra also an arid climate phase associated with Microlithic assemblage has been identified during the terminal Pleistocene.

As the Holocene started, the southwest monsoon was rapidly strengthened. Many marginal arid regions became habitable for both animals and human communities. In Western India, microlithic sites of all kinds abound everywhere except in the most arid central parts of the desert. As in peninsular India they take the form of small camping places, semi-permanent settlements and multi-activity sites, usually on old fixed dunes or small hills and quite large factory sites to which nodules of chert and agate must have been carried many kilometres from their sources. A few sites have been excavated and Bagor in eastern Rajasthan, has shown a cultural sequence from Mesolithic to Chalcolithic, with C^{14} dates ranging from *c.* 7000 yrs ago forward. During this time the site changed from a Mesolithic camping place to a small Neolithic/Chalcolithic settlement.

The Neolithic culture with regional variation has been reported from almost all states of India except a few states like Maharashtra, Gujarat, Rajasthan, Goa etc. Four distinct Neolithic cultural zones have been identified. They are the Northern Neolithic, the Southern Neolithic, the Central Indian Neolithic and the Eastern Neolithic zone. The Northern Neolithic is best known from the evidences found in the sites of Burzahom

and Gufkral. The inhabitants were pit dwellers in the aceramic phase dated to 2900 B.C. and ceramic phase dated to 2500 B.C.

The South Indian Neolithic was primarily based upon cattle keeping and to some extent on the cultivation of a range of millets and some other crops. The settlements are located on the southern Deccan plateau. The ground and polished axes has an elongated triangular outline with a cylindrical section. Basalt is the most common raw material. There is a fine blade industry with regular blades made from blocks of chert. The economy was completely based on pastoralism supported by collection of wild grains until millets made their appearance sometime in the course of the third millennium B.C. (Allchin and Allchin 1997: 102-104). The best known sites are Kodekkal, Utnur, Palavoy, Budihal etc.

The most recent work on the South Indian Neolithic is the excavation conducted at Budihal on the Neolithic pastoral settlement with ash deposits. This site located in Shorapur taluka, Gulbarga district yielded pottery, lithic material belonging to the blade tool, and pecked and ground tool industries and faunal material representing both domestic and wild species. The excavation in the area also yielded a lot of bone artifacts. Dolerite granite/sandstone and other coarse-grained rocks were used for making pecked and ground stone tools. The artifact types included hammerstones, rubberstones, chopping tools and knives The fresh data inevitably led to the conclusion that the ashmound sites were true pastoral settlements where the garbage accumulating from the nocturnal penning of cattle and other domestic animals was dumped along with household refuse at one or two convenient spots in or close to the settlement and was periodically burnt. Eleven C^{14} dates have been obtained till now which prove that the Neolithic settlement of Budihal spanned the period between *c.* 4000 yrs B.P. - 3000 yrs B.P. (Paddayya 1993: 277-290).

In the Ganges valley/Vindhyan region the Neolithic appears to have developed out of the Mesolithic retaining many features such as the microlithic blade industry and the range of heavy stone tools; but it was distinguished by certain important new features including domestic cattle, whose bones are found increasingly along side those of wild cattle; large huts grouped round small cattle pens in which actual foot prints of cattle were found, and, most important, a form of cultivated rice. All these features were found at Mahagara, Koldihawa, Pachoh, Indari, Kunjhun etc. Handmade pottery of several types like cord-impressed pottery, plain red and plain black ware and a ware with deliberately roughened rusticated surfaces were reported. A further feature of this group of sites is the small flat ground stone axes, round or square outline. Stone axes, which are longer, more cylindrical in section and triangular in outline have been reported from the area. C^{14} dates are available from Chopani- Mando, Koldihawa and Mahagara. At Chopani-Mando, the earliest occurrence of wild rice is said to be in the final stage of the Mesolithic, dated to *c.* 6000 B.C. and cultivated rice occurs first at Neolithic sites such as Mahagara (6th to 7th millennium B.C.) (Allchin and Allchin 1997: 94-97).

In East India evidences of the Neolithic culture have been widely reported from Orissa, Bihar, West Bengal besides Northeast India. The best known site from Orissa is Kuchai. Evidences have also come from Golabai, Bonaigarh etc. Fourteen Neolithic tool types have been recorded which include axe, adze, chisel etc. Occurrence of Shouldered celts is a noteworthy feature of the Orissan Neolithic (Basa and Mohanty 2000). Chirand and Barudih are two well known Neolithic sites from Bihar. Evidences of the cultivation of rice have been found in these sites besides pottery and stone tools. The Neolithic artifacts from Bihar bear affinity with the southern peninsular and Eastern Neolithic traditions including south Chinese and southeast Asiatic (Narayan 1996). In West Bengal two distinct Neolithic cultural zones have been reported. The Neolithic culture of the southwestern zone is dominated by triangular axes with rounded butt end and having mostly lenticular and plano-convex cross-section, shouldered celts and the splayed axes. The ceramic industry consists of grey and pale red ware. The Neolithic

culture from Kalimpong in the northern corner of the state is dominated by rounded butt axes, splayed axe and perforated celts which brings it very close to the Neolithic culture of the Yunnan province of China (Datta 1992)

The Late/Terminal Pleistocene and Early Holocene cultures of Southeast Asia

Wilhelm G. Solheim II in 1969, while defining 'Southeast Asia' divided it into two distinct parts and identified the boundaries demarcating the region. According to him, mainland Southeast Asia is the area within the 30th Parallel or the Yantze River, south through Singapore. Island Southeast Asia included the islands off the coast of the mainland from Taiwan through the Andaman and Nicobar islands. The area extended up to Assam and Eastern India and to a portion of western New Guinea (Solheim 1969: 126-127) (Fig. 2).

Researches on the prehistoric past of the region started from the middle of the 19th century. After completing almost a century of research the archaeologist suggested that, like the rest of Eurasia and Africa, the original archaeological tradition in Southeast Asia, from which all subsequent cultures were derived, are based on manufacture of pebble tools. In accordance with the then accepted theory that human culture has evolved in a unilinear fashion, the early specialists believed that the original Asian archaeological cultures were based, as they were in Europe and Africa, on the manufacture of core tools. The original stimulus of the idea of a basal pebble tool culture in Southeast Asia was derived from archaeological and geological investigation in China (Pei 1931; Teilhard de Chardin 1932) and the Indian subcontinent (De Terra and Paterson 1936) early in the 20th century.

Hallam Movius, in 1948 after a period of research stated that the Asian core tools differed fundamentally from their European and African counterparts (Movius 1948: 329-420). That is, whereas the European and African core tools were handaxes fully shaped by bifacial flaking techniques, the Asian core tools were mainly rounded pebbles partially shaped by unifacial or

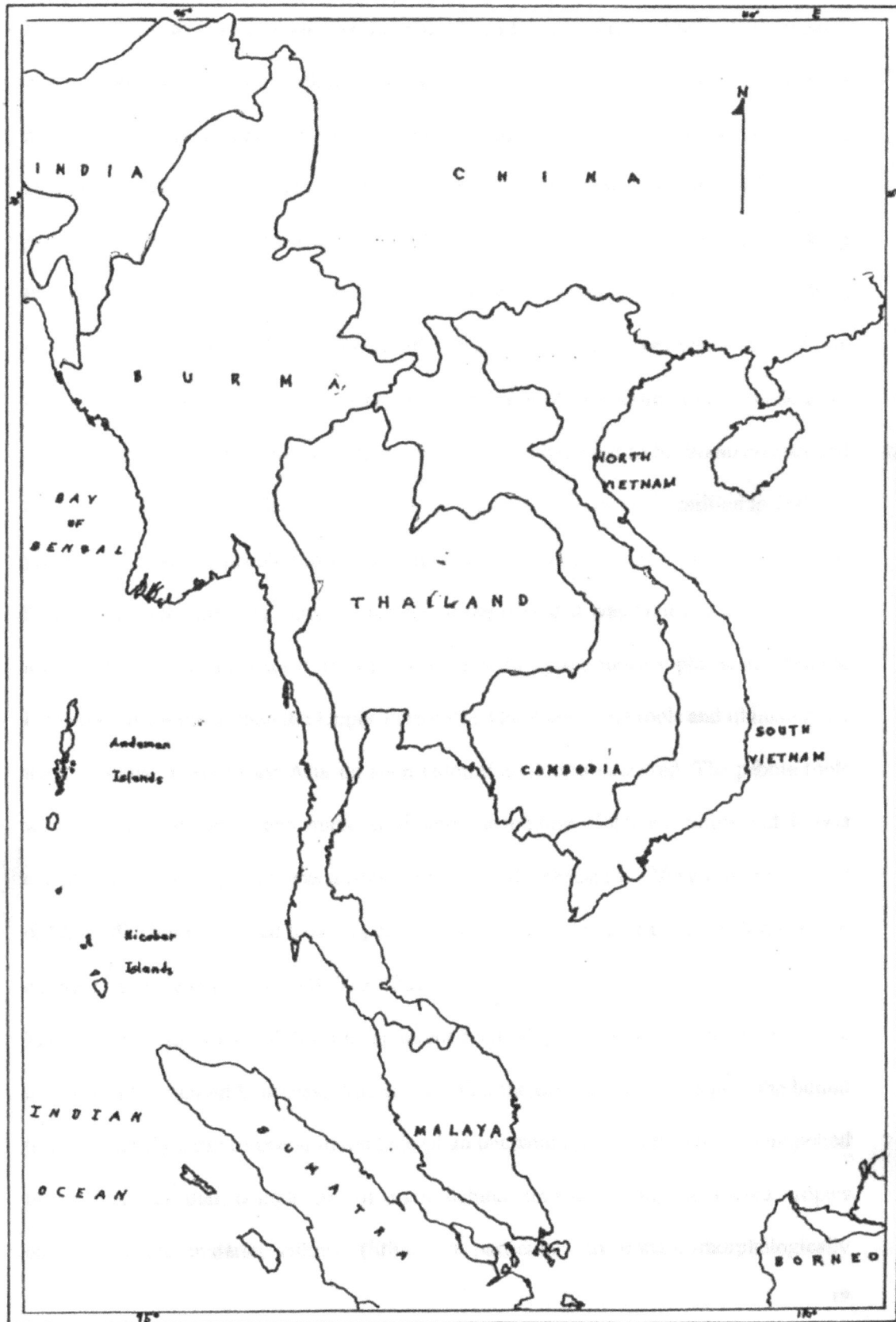

Figure 2: Map of Southeast Asia

bifacial flaking techniques. To emphasize this contrast with the African and European handaxe traditions, Movius grouped the Burmese finds, which he labelled as the early Anyathian, as well as the finds from Java, which Von Koenigswald (1936) labelled as the Patjitanian, and also finds from northwestern India and northern China, under a single core tool complex of South Asia and the Far East. Thus, was born the concept of the "Movius Line" which is a geographical boundary extending through Northern India that separates two long lasting Palaeolithic cultures. West of the line are found collections of tools with a high percentage of symmetrical and consistently proportioned hand axes while the tools on the eastern side classified as choppers and chopping tools are more crudely made tools on river pebbles. The authors of both the industries are believed to be *Homo erectus* and are of similar age. The Acheulean tools of the west were dated to 1.5 million to 200,000 years and the eastern pebble tools were dated to 1 million to 200,000 years. For reasons best known to the archaeological fraternity of the period it was believed that while the lower Palaeolithic Acheulean in Europe was replaced by the more sophisticated Middle Palaeolithic flake tools, then the Upper Palaeolithic blade and bone tools and ultimately by the microliths, in Southeast Asia no such cultural evolution occurred. The pebble tools were believed to have been made well into the middle Holocene times and it was concluded that the Far East was a region of 'cultural retardation'. Very primitive forms of Early Man were believed to have persisted in the east long after the types had become extinct elsewhere (Movius 1948: 329-420).

The explanations provided for the apparent technological conservatism in the lithic industries of mainland Southeast Asia are:

(1) that the cultures had to adapt to the humid tropics at a very early time and in the face of an unchanging climate were not compelled to change;

(2) that complexity of man habitat interaction in the humid tropics encouraged the material culture (lithics in particular) to remain morphologically unpatterned, simple, amorphous and undifferentiated; and

(3) that our view of the prehistoric tropical cultures is seriously skewed by the invisibility (because of the lack of organic preservation) of the most significant part of the material culture actually in use by the prehistoric peoples.

The purported existence of a long lasting core tool tradition in mainland Southeast Asia is based on three propositions:

(1) core tool industries are already present in Asia by the Middle Pleistocene, as evidenced in India (Soanian), Java (Patjitanian), Burma (Early Anyathian), and north China (Choukoutienian);

(2) in mainland Southeast Asia these industries, representing a single complex or tradition, continued to flourish throughout the middle and upper Pleistocene, as evidenced by archaeological finds from Malaysia (Tampanian), various surface finds from Thailand, Cambodia, Vietnam; and

(3) Hoabinhian, a pebble tool industry, represents a direct historical continuity into early Holocene times of this purported Middle and Upper Pleistocene tradition.

The Hoabinhian discovered by Madeline Colani in Vietnam during 1926-1930 was initially identified as a pebble tool industry. Very soon similar sites were discovered in Laos, Malaysia, Indonesia, Thailand etc. and the industry received a pan-Southeast Asian status. The Bacsonian and the Sonvian are two other industries from Vietnam almost belonging to the same time period. The former is also a pebble tool industry but with a greater frequency of axes with polished edges called the Bacsonian Axe while the Sonvian differs from the Hoabinhian because of the absence of the Sumatralith, the discoid, elliptical or amygdaloid pebbles cut on one face and retaining the cortex on the other. It is one of the characteristic tool type of the Hoabinhian. Besides this the other types of tools belonging to the

Hoabinhian techno-complex are bifacially flaked pebble tools of similar shape, truncated pebble tools (Short axe or *haches courts*), edge ground axes and a large quantity of utilized flakes, blades, hammerstones and cores (Gorman 1970; Bellwood 1982). Botanical evidence found in association with Hoabinhian tools in Spirit Cave, Northern Thailand excavated by Gorman further sanctified this techno-complex. Colani had reported it as a post-Pleistocene Mesolithic culture but the dates from Spirit Cave indicated that the culture dates back to the terminal Pleistocene period. The radiocarbon determinations mainly from *in situ* charcoal deposits indicate that the shelter was occupied from about 12,000 B.P. to about 7,500 B.P. These pebble tool industries were the major attraction of the archaeologist working in the region for a very long time.

But it was soon noticed that in many of the sites with the pebble tools there was a certain percentage of probably utilized flakes also which have been often ignored. Chinese archaeologists now emphasize that locality I Choukoutien assigned to the Middle Pleistocene period contains 71.3% flake tools. If there is some reason to doubt the existence of the East and Southeast Asian Chopper-Chopping tool complex dating back to the Middle Pleistocene, there is even more reason to question its existence in the Upper Pleistocene. Turning first to Insular Southeast Asia, we find that most, if not all, Upper Pleistocene archaeological sites like Niah, Tabon, Lang Rongrien etc. that are securely dated are characterized by flake tools. Although a few core or pebble tools are present, such implements are never a major element in any of the assemblages. For example, the lowermost levels at Niah cave, the first radiocarbon dated Pleistocene archaeological site in Southeast Asia, produced a handful of unmodified flakes, but no core tools. Pebble tools and pebble implements together account for only 12% of the Phase II assemblage, dated to about 40,000 years ago, 41% of the Phase III assemblage, dating to about 30,000 years ago, and 11.7% of all of the entire lithic assemblage of Niah Cave. Excavation at Tabon cave on Palawan Island, Philippines likewise revealed a predominance of flake tools produced by percussion flaking techniques. Along the southern edge of mainland Southeast Asia the late Pleistocene industries in south China were also clearly based on the production of flake tools, and by relatively advanced stone working techniques. The only Upper Pleistocene representative of Movius's original Chopper-Chopping tool complex in Southeast Asia is the Late Anyathian of Burma, dated by geological correlation and degree of weathering of the stone implements.

From Niah Cave, Sarawak and Tabon caves of Philippines we have the earliest dated prehistoric cultural sequences of cave deposits with C^{14} dates going back to *c.* 40,000 B.P. and 30,000 B.P. respectively (Harrisson 1967: 95; Fox 1970: 18). Late Pleistocene flake traditions are better known from Tabon cave, Palawan where Fox (1970) has recovered a good sequence of artifacts and bones from about 40,000-9000 B.P. Fox has analysed the material in terms of five sequential flake assemblages which show very little change over time and are difficult to characterize in any positive way. Flakes are generally large, 80 per cent of one sample being more then 5 cm long and made of a coarse brown chert, from pebbles whose cortex often remains on the flake. Although some flakes were obviously used, less than one percent has any secondary modification and these, according to Fox, defy easy classification into types based on morphology or the positioning of retouch. These tools can best be described as flat, multi-edged scrapers: with a single implement having concave, convex, straight working edges and occasionally small prepared notches. Tabon and Niah both show a long continuity of a very simple, even primitive flake tool tradition in the late Pleistocene, with the absence of specialized forms and core tools. The Niah cave, west of Borneo is located in an isolated hill called Gunong Subis, an island of limestone set in the sub-coastal sandstone plain, 300 miles up the coast from Kuching. It is 800 feet wide and over 200 feet high. Excavations conducted by the Sarawak Museum in the later part of 1950s helped archaeologists to construct the prehistoric picture of Niah. It is as shown below:

Phase	Characteristic	Approx. Niah start date	Method of dating
Middle Palaeolithic	'Mid Sohan' flake	?40-50-000 B.C.	Flake below C^{14}
Upper Palaeolithic	Chopping tools and large flakes	?35,000 B.C.	Strata with C^{14}
Upper Palaeolithic	Smaller flakes	25-30,000 B.C.	C^{14}
Palaeo-Mesolithic	Advanced flakes	10,000 B.C.	C^{14} and stratification
Mesolithic	Edgeground tools. Melanoid dentitions	c. 7000 B.C.	Stratification
Neolithic	'Round axe'	c. 4000 B.C. (or later)	Stratification and Doubtful comparison.
Neolithic	Quadrangular adzes, Mongoloid dentitions, pottery, mats, nets etc.	c. 1000 B.C.	Stratification: area and contemporary comparisons
Chalcolithic	'Soft tools' in stone, slightbronze, elaborate pottery beads.	c. A.D. 0	Association and 'Dongs' on culture traces
Early Iron	Iron tools, imported ceramics, glass beads etc.	A.D. 700 (until A.D. 1300)	Dated T'ang. coins and ceramics

In Niah the first evidence of Palaeolithic material in Southeast Asia was found. Besides choppers four types of flakes have been classified. The first type is the mid-Sohan flake, which is rough and crude, but notably thin, wide and sharp, with a coarsely faceted butt. The second category constitutes big rough primary flakes, very variable and nearly always fairly well shaped and bladed. A few are dressed, but there is no secondary working. The third type is made up of smaller, usually less crude flakes and the fourth group consists of flakes, which have been carefully reworked.

Between the clearly Palaeolithic rough flakes on the one hand and quite sophisticated polished Neolithic tools on the other there is a rather dense band of intermediate material which can reasonably, be treated as Mesolithic and Palaeo-Mesolithic (transitional) in a broad sense at Niah. This includes:

(i)   worked flakes of advanced kind

(ii) edge-ground axes, sometimes massive, always carefully and symmetrically worked on a pebble surface; the butt end commonly struck and flaked bifacially to a rough point.

(iii) edge-ground adzes, usually smaller pebbles: sometimes ground all over to shape, almost to the extent of polishing.

All artifacts of this period at Niah are dissimilar from the usual Asian forms.

An earlier Neolithic, merging downward into 'Mesolithic', is characterized by round axes, distinctly stratified at Niah. For the first time both quadrangular and round tools have been found clearly together. The quadrangular tools from Niah are of a kind common through the islands and on the mainland from the north into China. These tools are associated with a variety of earthen wares (Harrisson 1959: 1-7).

The Neolithic in the region is marked by the occurrence of cord-marked pottery and shouldered celts besides the quadrangular adzes and polished celts with lenticular cross-section. From Ban Kao, Sai Yok and Don Noi in western Thailand the best evidences have come of the Neolithic of the region which is usually defined as a middle Holocene industry.

Thus, it is clear that in Southeast Asia two major archaeological traditions coexisted during the Late Pleistocene. One was flake tool tradition that evolved in South China by 40,000 or 50,000 yrs ago which subsequently spread to island Southeast Asia, by passing present-day mainland Southeast Asia via the then exposed Sunda shelf. The other was the pebble tool tradition developed much earlier by pre-*Homo sapiens* that was distributed throughout mainland Southeast Asia from Vietnam to Burma and Malaysia. Although the core tool tradition began earlier, and was subsequently replaced by a flake tool tradition in South China and island Southeast Asia it continued with only slight modifications in mainland Southeast Asia throughout the Pleistocene and the early Holocene. Hoabinhian represents the early Holocene facies of this tradition, as well the archaeological stage from which the Neolithic cultures of Southeast Asia developed. The results of the recent excavations at Lang Rongrien rockshelter in Southwestern Thailand, taken together with other recent evidence from Southeast Asia, indicate that:

(1) disregarding the question of the core tool industries of the middle Pleistocene for which we find little good confirmation at least the Upper Pleistocene archaeological assemblages throughout East and Southeast Asia were primarily flake industries;

(2) the level of technology exhibited by the Upper Pleistocene industries were rather advanced in that such techniques as the use of the burin blow, blade or possibly micro blade manufacture, retouching by the removal of long parallel sided flakes from the margins of tools were consistently employed, despite the predominance of percussion flaking;

(3) Hoabinhian does not demonstrate a cultural continuity from the known upper Pleistocene cultures of southeast Asia;

(4) Hoabinhian therefore represents a major change in technology at the end of the upper Pleistocene or beginning of the early Holocene; and

(5) although the most recent ecological explanations for the nature of the Hoabinhian material culture are reasonable, we must not treat them as apologies for seeming cultural stagnation but rather as examples of ecological principles against which to examine the actual differences we observe in the region's archaeological remains.

If the Hoabinhian represents a significant departure in the course of development of early Southeast Asian technology, then change, not continuity, marks the transition from Late Pleistocene to early Holocene archaeological complexes in mainland Southeast Asia. The reasons for change may well be ecological conditions changed and therefore the material culture changed to adapt to the new ecological conditions. However, given the general synchronicity of the earliest Hoabinhian sites, the environmental change must have been a broad scale one, occurring simultaneously in several habitats stretching from the humid tropics to the warm temperate regions of Southeast Asia, as well as along coast, in river valleys, and in mountainous regions. Furthermore, given our current understanding of the Hoabinhian, the onset of the change must have occurred sometime after 25,000 years ago, but somewhat prior to the 13th millennium B.P. the earliest substantiated dates for the complex (Anderson 1990: 67-74).

In several regions of Southeast Asia Hoabinhian and non-Hoabinhian assemblages, appear to have been contemporaneous. In northern Vietnam these may include Hoabinhaian and the Bacsonian and in Thailand it may include the Hoabinhian and the flake tool assemblage. In Sumatra several different contemporaneous industries have been reported. These finds in Southeast Asia suggest greater variability in the late Pleistocene industries of the region than was hitherto suspected.

As early as 1866, the first report of archaeological discoveries made in Assam appeared in 'Athaneum'of London in the form of an article 'The stone age tools in upper Assam' by Sir John Lubbock. From then on several notable collections of stone age antiquities were made in this area.

Among these the discovery of polished stone axes from Nagaland by Hutton, from Garo hills by Walkar, from North Cachar hills by Hutton and Mills and Sadiya frontier tract by Mills, and Pawsay are noteworthy. Subsequent scholars have studied and catalogued this material preserved in various museums. Notable studies are the ones made by A.H. Dani (1960) and T.C. Sharma (1966a). In Dani's work the whole of the northeast was divided into five classes and one miscellaneous class and in T.C. Sharma's works an inventory of tools from different localities was provided. The first detailed study of the tools from Garo hills was provided in this study. About 850 tools were selected for this study from different localities. These were divided into 19 types of which 7 were types of chipped stone implements and 12 were types of fully ground stone implements. The sites selected for study are Rongram, Rengchanggiri, Ronngchigiri, Ronchu-gate, Rambhagiri, Chitra, Tura and Phulbari. The Pitt Rivers museum collection was restudied. A classified inventory of the Neolithic tool types of Garo hills was provided. The inventory is reproduced below:

Chipped Stone implements

(1) Tools of Handaxe type
(2) Choppers and scrapers
(3) Simple flakes
(4) Blade core
(5) Tanged lance-head
(6) Chipped celts (axes and hoes)
(7) Broad axes.

Fully ground implements

(1) Flat celts
    i. Long variety
    ii. Short variety

(2) Tanged or shouldered celts
    a. Curvilinear variety
        i. single shouldered
        ii. double shouldered

(3)   Notched or waisted celts
(4)   Small celts
(5)   Quadrangular axes
(6)   Pointed Butt Indian axe type
(7)   Chisels
(8)   Wedges or cold chisels
(9)   Lance-head
(10)   Large and thin celts
(11)   Giant celts
(12)   Hammers
(13)   Broken celts and nondescript types

Two separate industrial traditions were identified. The tools made by flaking technique were taken to represent the first and probably the earlier tradition. The ground stone tools represent the second tradition. The convex grinding resulting in lenticular cross-section seems to be the norm in this area. Tools showing flat grinding and rectangular sections are very rare. This study helped northeast India to achieve a firm place on the prehistoric map of the world.

In 1972 H.C. Sharma from the Department of Anthropology of the Gauhati University produced the first thesis specifically on the 'Stone Age Cultures of Garo Hills'. The main objective of this work was to study the lithic tools from Garo Hills, which typologically did not belong to the Neolithic period. Pleistocene sediments in the valleys of the rivers Rongram and Simsang, two major rivers of the area, were examined for the first time. A chronological framework of the Stone Age cultures of northeast India was constructed. It is as follows:

Geological age	Stratigraphy	Stone industries	Cultural Phase
Holocene	Upper silt	Series IV (Microlithic Industry)	Late Stone Age
Late Pleistocene?	?	Series III (Blade Industry) Series II (flake Industry)	Late-middle Stone Age Early-middle Stone Age
Middle Pleistocene	Cemented coarse gravel	Series I (Hand-axe Cleaver Industry	Early Stone Age

In 1980 D.K. Medhi from Deccan College, in his thesis 'Quaternary History of the Garo Hills, Meghalaya' forwarded the view that a study of the Quaternary history of this region primarily involves the interplay between the Pleistocene glacial and inter-glacial conditions prevailing in the Himalayas and the variations in the intensity of the tropical monsoon circulation originating in the Indian Ocean. In order to understand the pattern of this complex weather machine he says it is necessary to analyse the evidence prescribed in the deeply entrenched valleys of the Garo hills and then try to project these results against more recently acquired data of quaternary environmental changes in the tropical and sub- tropical world. He recorded four erosional surfaces (1200-100 m, 900 m, 700 m and 600 m) in Garo hills. His conclusions were that surfaces in Garo hills are definitely not older than the late Tertiary period. The relative chronology of the various geomorphic events in the Garo Hills was attempted as shown in the following table:

Geomorphic features	Probable age
1. Younger alluvial fill (T3)	Sub- recent (Holocene)
Disconformity represented by erosion of the older fill and by the formation of erosional terraces on the older fill (as at Rongram IB site)	
2. Older fill (T2)	Late Quaternary (Late Pleistocene)
Discomformity represented by bedrock incision	
3. Ferruginous conglomerate (T1)	Early Quaternary (Early - mid Pleistocene)
Unconformity	
4. Erosional surfaces developed on Archaeans and early Tertiary Formation	Late Tertiary and Early Quaternary

Medhi's laboratory studies indicated that seasonally flowing bedload streams deposited T1. The late Quaternary alluvial fill or T2 is represented predominantly by oxidized reddish brown alluvium. The younger alluvium or T3 has been deposited in a low energy floodplain environment. Both his field and laboratory studies show that for some reason not yet fully understood there was excessive soil stripping during the late Quaternary in the Garo hills. Mineralogical and chemical characters of the late Quaternary alluvium and its comparison with soils and alluvium of the sub-recent period show that the climate during this period was hot tropical monsoonic.

In 1987 Minarva Sonowal from the Department of Anthropology, Gauhati University made a study of the flake and blade industries of Garo hills, Meghalaya. The primary aim of this study was to identify the sites of the flake tool and blade tool industries reported from Garo hills and to examine in detail and identify the stone tool techniques applied in preparation of flake and blade tools in Garo Hills. This study was a very exhaustive study, which established the presence of a blade-flake tool tradition in Garo Hills.

In 1995 Hari Chandra Mahanta from the same department produced a Ph.D. thesis entitled 'A study on the Stone Age Cultures of Selbalgiri, West Garo Hills Meghalaya'. The main aim of the study was to draw a concrete profile of either the typo-technological evolution or the chronological ordering of the tool assemblages of the area. Tools belonging to Palaeolithic, Mesolithic and Neolithic cultures were identified. A chrono-cultural model of Selbalgiri lithic industry is provided below:

Geological Era	Cultural sequence	Stratigraphic units	Stone Industry	Geological period
Quaternary	Neolithic	Conspicuous erosional phase with warm humid climate, enhancement of forest coverage. Hoabinhian and Neolithic cultural evidences appeared in the area.	Fully ground tools, chipped and Ground tools, pottery.	Holocene

	Mesolithic	Unit-III (gravel III, silt III) Unit-II (gravel II, silt II)	Microlithic flake blade industry. Special variety tools (Hoabinhian)	Early Holocene Late Pleistocene
	Upper Palaeolithic	Conspicuous aggradation in suitable basins by both older and younger sediments.	Blade tool industry	Late or Upper- Middle Pleistocene
	Middle Palaeolithic	Cold dry Climate with reduction of forest coverage. Palaeolithic cultural evidence appeared in the area. Unit II (gravel III, silt II) Unit I (gravel II, silt I)	Flake tool industry	
	?	Erosional surfaces developed sometimes filled with older alluvium.	?	Early-Mid Pleistocene.

The wide variety of the artifact types made Garo hills a very prospective area for further research. The profuse distribution of sites all over the landscape provided enough scope to the researcher to deal with a variety of sites. In these studies the workers have constantly forwarded relative chronologies of the lithic assemblages of Garo hills on the basis of typology. Typological dating has not been corroborated by data on the contextual origin of the tools. Most of the sites have been often referred as surface sites and the data has been analysed overlooking the limitations of surface data. Site formation processes that might have acted on the assemblages have completely been ignored. Settlement pattern of the possible inhabitants, which might have affected the distribution of the data on the landscape, has also not been studied. Thus, though the typological inventory of the tool assemblage is quite rich, the ages assigned to each type have been a topic of controversy. Workers from the area have also attempted to relatively date the artifacts comparing them with similar finds from other parts of India and Southeast Asia. These studies are also not free from doubts because it has still not been confirmed that similar palaeo-climatic conditions persisted in the two areas between which comparisons have been made and similar cultural evolution occurred in the two areas. Thus, it is very difficult to conclude that affinities in tool typology are the result of the development of similar cultures during the same time period.

The type of data to be interpreted includes the lithic artifacts, the alluvial mounds or deposits within which the artifacts are found and the present lifestyle of the inhabitants of the area. From the studies done till now it seems that the landscape witnessed much human activity during the Late/Terminal Pleistocene period. Majority of the tools typologically seems to belong to the Late/Terminal Pleistocene-Early Holocene period. So, in the present study much emphasis will be laid on the man-land relationship prevailing in and around Ganol-Rongram valley in particular, and Northeast India, other parts of India and Southeast Asia in general.

THE STUDY AREA

The Ganol and Rongram river valleys lying between 25° 5` E Lat. and 90°N Longitude, is located in the western side of the Garo hills district of Meghalaya, India. This district lying between 25° 9` and 26° 1`N and between 89° 49` and 91° 2` E covers an area of 8000 sq kms.

It is bounded on the north by the Goalpara district of Assam; on the east by the Khasi and Jayantia hills; and on the west and north by Bangladesh (Fig. 3).

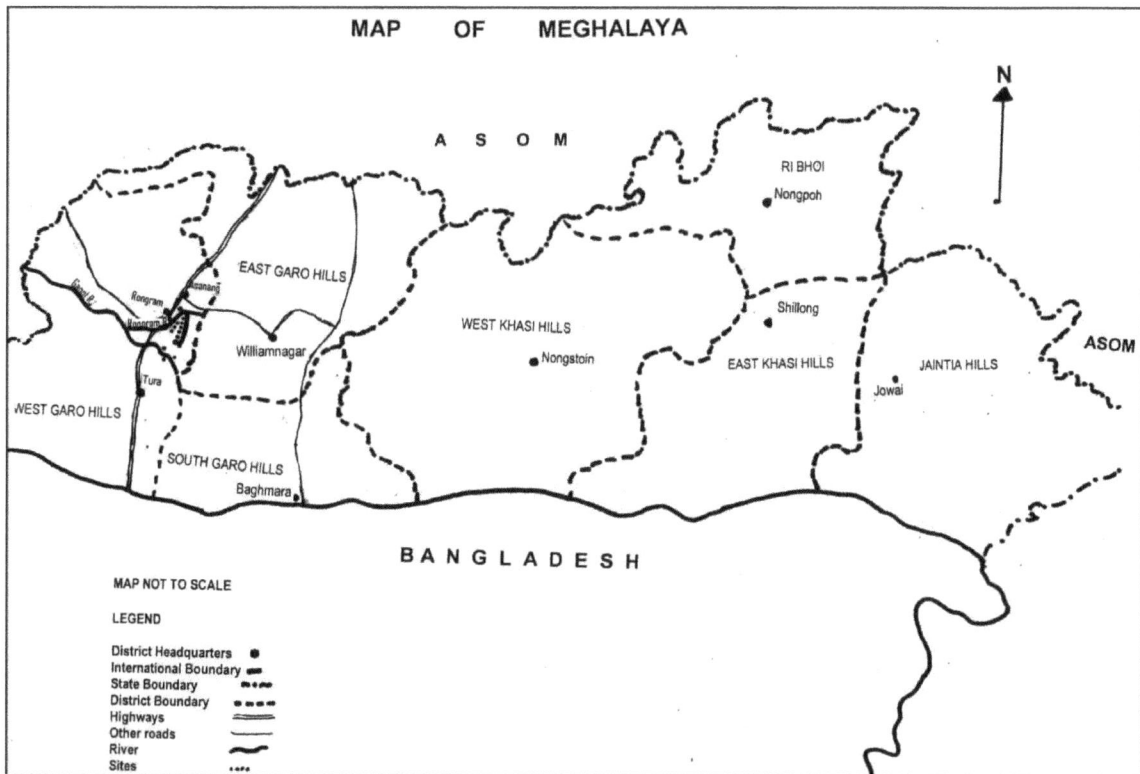

Figure 3: Map of Meghalaya Showing sites

The Ganol is the main river in the valley and the Rongram and the Rongkhon are its two tributaries. No sites were marked in the Rongkhon Valley, which has a steep gradient, so deposition is less. Majority of the sites are in the Rongram valley with a very thick alluvial deposit. There are number of first and second order streams. Important among them are the Selbal Chiring, Michima Chiring, the Mokbol Chiring, and the Ida Chiring. The average distances between these streams are one to two kms. They are seasonal but in certain stretches even in the driest season some water is present.

The drainage is dendritic. The streams flow in an extraordinarily straight course evidently along joints and faults. Structures, faults and monoclines in the sedimentary rocks mostly control the streams. Almost all the streams including the two main rivers flow on the gneissic bedrock with very less deposition seen on the riverbed.

It falls under the tropical climatic zone and experiences heavy monsoonic rainfall.

Three types of vegetation have been identified. They are:

(1) Tropical Evergreen forest

(2) Tropical moist deciduous forest and

(3) Savannas and bamboo forests

The area under study falls in the West Garo Hills district The oldest rocks found in the area belong to the Archaean gneissic complex whose age is estimated to be about 3600 million years. The gneisses intruded by granitods and younger intrusives formed the basement over which the sediments of Gondwana and Tertiary were deposited. A number of un-decomposed dykes of doleritic and basaltic composition intrude the gneisses in the form of sills and dykes. They are usually thin and many are less than 5 m wide. Most of the prominent basic intrusives in the area are in general concordant to the foliation in gneisses.

The Gondwana sediments are dated to about 350 million years. The older metabasics and metasedimentaries such as hornblende schist, Quartz-sericite-schicst is found as rafts and enclaves within the migmatites and granitoids. Subsequently, all these rocks have been nearly homogenised by regional metamorphism and granitisation. Lower Gondwana are represented by conglomerates and pebble beds, gritty sandstones, shells and many carbonaceous shale horizons which lies on the Archaean gneiss. There are two formations Talchir and Kaharbari, of the lower Gondwana sediments. In the study area un-decomposed to partly decomposed feldspar in sediments of Kaharbari formation indicates a cold temperate climate. Evidence of the first fluvio-lacustrine sedimentation in the area can be assumed from the lower Gondwana beds containing carbonaceous shale and coal. Gondwana sediments were deposited on an uneven undulating gneissic platform. The deposition of Tura sandstone member begins with the development of deltaic complex. The sandstone unit of Tura sandstone member is dominant medium to coarse, loose, friable, angular too subangular but gravely to pebbly at places and at places feldspatic. Colour of the sandstone on fresh surfaces is light grayish brown to reddish. The lower part is inter-bedded with clay and upper with greyish shale and carbonaceous shale having laminae and streaks of coal material. Tura sandstone member is lying over unconformably or in juxtaposition with the faulted contacts with basement Gneissises and marks the onset of Tertiary sedimentation in the area. Both trough and planar cross bedding and herringbone structure in the Tura sandstone member indicates beach environment. Many indigenous carbonised plant remains in Tura sandstone member indicates near shore environment. It is composed of clasts of sandstone, feldspar, shale, and clay in the matrix of feldspathic sandstone. This formation has been dated to about 65 million years.

Conglomerates overlie the Tura sandstone member in the study area. Two distinct formations of conglomerates have been marked. They are Boldamgiri formation and Chengapara formation. In the study area the conglomerate is composed of poorly cemented loose, fine micaceous sandstone, siltstone, mudstone and clay. But in the Rongram I.B. section a ferricretised section of this formation is visible. On this conglomerates which is often referred as a pebbly horizon alluvial filling has taken place, which is a fluvatile deposit. The alluvium is of two types. The recent or the younger alluvium is yellowish brown in colour while the older alluvium is reddish brown in colour. The thickness of the alluvium varies from two meters to ten meters.

A tentative sequence of the various rock units mapped in the study area is as follows (Fig. 4):

Group	Formation	Lithofacies	Age
Newer alluvium		Unconsolidated sand and silt	Recent and sub-recent Holocene
Older alluvium			Pleistocene
Garo group	Baghmara formation	Conglomerate, feldspatic sandstone, mudsto-neshale and minor fossil wood	Oligocene Miocene
Lower Gondwana	Talchir formation	Conglomerates with greenish matrix.	
Archaean Gneissic complex		Granitiod Gneiss	

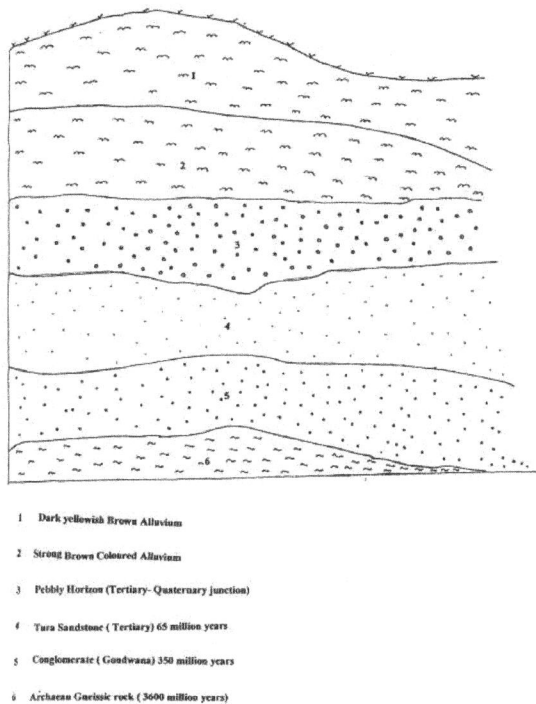

1   Dark yellowish Brown Alluvium

2   Strong Brown Coloured Alluvium

3   Pebbly Horizon (Tertiary- Quaternary junction)

4   Tura Sandstone (Tertiary) 65 million years

5   Conglomerate (Gondwana) 350 million years

6   Archaean Gneissic rock (3600 million years)

Figure 4: Geological History of the area Represented by an Idealised Section: Rongram IB

Local environmental factors that influenced original site selection.

Factors likely to influence human habitation in an area are proximity to water and high yield/low-cost food resources, accessibility, protection from bad weather and environmental hazards, dry ground surface, defensibility, and availability of building materials (Hassan 1985: 95). Availability of these resources depends on the local environment. An environment is a subdivision of the earth's surface distinguished and delimited on the basis of physical, chemical, and or biological criteria (Hassan 1985: 87). It can be considered as a dynamic factor in the analysis of archaeological context. Human culture is often defined as the durable material expression of an adaptation to an environment, human as well as physiographical, that enabled a society to survive and develop (Childe 1951: 16). Ecological archaeology, the study of the interrelationship between human groups and their habitats, is one of the key approaches to archaeology today. In fact the ultimate goal of archaeology has been identified as the determination of interrelationship between culture and environment,

emphasising archaeological research directed towards a fuller understanding of the human ecology of prehistoric cultures (Butzer 1964: vii, 5). Thus, a fuller understanding of the environment, to which the authors of the culture in Garo hills area under study adapted is necessary.

Study of ancient landscape is important for knowing about the location of settlements and the spatial organisation of food-getting activities. Past climatic changes are of interest because of the potential effects of climatic change on food resources and mode of cultural adaptation. Archaeologists often concentrate on sites, but since human activities are distributed over a range or territory surrounding a site, a regional approach to palaeoenvironmental reconstruction is necessary. Palaeoenvironments may be classified according to climatic-geologic systems; geomorphic units or landscapes and sedimentary (depositional) environments (Hassan 1985: 98). The long term characteristics of an environment (climatic stability, fluctuations, secular changes) are crucial for interpreting certain cultural changes. The identification of reciprocal interactions between people and environment is crucial in understanding prehistoric cultural change, especially which has occurred since the terminal Pleistocene (Hassan 1985: 99).

The sedimentary record of the study area has been outlined above. Lithic artifacts the only evidence of the prehistoric occupation of the area occur within the alluvial deposit whose average thickness varies between 1 and 10 m (Plate 3). Alluvial terraces are formed when a floodplain is abandoned through valley incision, thereby isolating the terrace surface from flooding. The deposition of this large amount of alluvium in the upper and middle courses of the river does not usually take place. This extremely fertile alluvial deposits seems to be one of the prime factors, which influenced selection of this area for habitation. This alluvial stretch has supported people from time immemorial. These deposits look like low hillocks with rounded top, cut through by tributaries of the Ganol, and numerous firsts order and second order streams. An attempt is made to understand the origin and formation of this geomorphic unit, which can provide some information on the past climatic conditions of the area, and help us to understand man-environment relationship that existed in the past. An analysis will also be made to examine if the likely factors influencing human habitation in an area existed within the Ganol-Rongram valley.

Plate 3: Rounded top Alluvial Deposits

The Quaternary is the only geological period of interest to archaeologists, as human culture, originated during this period. The Quaternary processes and events in Northeast India have been profoundly influenced by the uplift of the Himalayas and climatic oscillations. In parts of north and northeast India, the Quaternary fluvial, fluvio-lacustrine, lacustrine, fluvio-glacial and glacial sediments are broadly related to the three cycles of sedimentation. The first cycle of sedimentation formed part of the late Neogene sedimentation in the Siwalik basin or the foredeep that continued into the Lower Pleistocene. It terminated with the last phase of the Himalayan orogeny (HO-4) during the early Middle Pleistocene. The second cycle was initiated in Middle Pleistocene in the Indo-Gangetic and Brahmaputra basins of the sub-Himalayan and Arakan Youma Mountains and terminated in the Upper Pleistocene. It continued in some smaller basins/lakes. The third cycle commenced at the advent of the Holocene and is still continuing. In the literature dealing with the sub-continent the Quaternary deposits of the Ganga-Brahmaputra-Narmada-Son were classified as Newer and Older Alluvium. Medlicott (1865) suggested a fluvial origin for the Older Alluvium. He described the Older Alluvium as 'massive ochreous clay' more or less sandy, differing from silt and sandy deposits of delta and inland/upland river course (Newer Alluvium). Coulson (1942), described the detached outcrops of Older Alluvium from the parts of Brahmaputra valley as 'Red Bank'- which is an apt term for the highly oxidized ochreous formation. In the Brahmaputra valley and adjacent valleys in parts of Assam, Arunachal Pradesh and Meghalaya fringe areas, generally four terraces have been mapped. The fluvial terrace deposit (T1), which is dissected, highly oxidized orange to dark brown colour, and mapped in the southeastern most corner of Assam, along Tipang *nala* has given an age of 38,020 ± 2,230 B.P., at Singra, 32,540 ± 130 B.P. in Lakhimpur District in the northern bank of Brahmaputra (Ramesh 1999: 13-35).

On the northern fringe of the Meghalaya plateau, the Quaternary sediments lie directly on the eroded basement of the Precambrian rocks. The geological record of the long stretch of time (Cambrian to Pliocene) is missing, necessitating the inference that the area formed an upland during this time interval and underwent continuous denudation. The Quaternary was heralded by a dramatic change in the palaeogeographic situation. Large-scale crustal movements, which caused morphotectonic uplift of the Himalayan orogen, had simultaneously buckled up the Precambrian massif of Meghalaya, triggering a phase of continental fluviatile sedimentation in the foredeep basin. Rejuvenated fracture controlled drainage system of Meghalaya denuded the soil cover, eroded the basement rocks, and transported the sediments onto the foredeep basin. The record of this episode of filling of the basin and subsequent evolution of the alluvial landscape is preserved in this terrain.

Morphostratigraphic mapping of about 1500 sq. km area in the lower Brahmaputra valley fringing the northern slopes of the Meghalaya plateau has distinctly brought out the deposition pattern of a sequence of four Quaternary morphostratigraphic units and a Precambrian rocky unit. The Quaternary land formation evolved through four distinct phases of fluvial sedimentation punctuated by degradational (erosional) breaks. But

18

there is a definite indication of break in the continuity of the Pleistocene sedimentation possibly due to base level lowering (i.e. eustatic causes). This evidence was collected from the Phutamati area in North Garo hills, bordering the northern slopes of Meghalaya plateau where partial erosion of the surface indicates a break. A subsequent rise in the base level must have caused the deposition of the Chibimang formation, a phase which just preceded the Holocene. But this seems to be short lived, as suggested by the minor thickness of this formation. During the Holocene large-scale valley fill took place, triggered by major eustatic changes coupled with climatic amelioration. The Holocene valley fills begins with coarse sediments, gradually ending up in a fining upward sequence. During the later part of the Pleistocene a definite decline in precipitation is envisaged (Sinha *et al*. 1983: 39-47).

These evidences from northern Garo Hills, which physiographically is similar to the rest of Garo Hills today, make it clear that climatic fluctuations during the Pleistocene affected the palaeogeographic situation of the study area which is in Central Garo hills, between the Tura range of mountains in the south and the Arbella range of mountains in the northeast. The Tura range constitutes a horst and the area is a subsided basin dissected by faults striking ESE-WNW, EW, N-W and NNW-SSE. The buckling up of the Precambrian massif of Meghalaya with the morphotectonic upliftment of the Himalayas triggered denudation of the soil cover from the two mountain ranges, which was deposited in the foredeep basin. The basin dissected by faults is like a trough, which was filled up by the eroded and transported sediments. Drainage system, as controlled by rejuvenated fracture in the area eroded the basement rocks, cut through the sediments, transporting and depositing them. This must have been one of the processes by which the Ganol-Rongram basin have got filled up, resulting in the unusually heavy deposition of alluvium in the upper and middle course of the river. Sedimentological analysis of the alluvium collected from three sites located at different contour levels show that the gravels present within the silt are very angular. This proves that the material has not been transported from a very long distance. Thus, denudation of the soil cover from the two mountain ranges, as a result of crustal movements during the Quaternary, resulted in the formation of the alluvial mounds.

A second explanation based on the study of palaeoclimate from different parts of the world provides us clues about the alluvial deposits in the upper and middle courses of the river and also on the possible palaeoclimatic condition of the area under study. During the Pleistocene, a succession of arid and pluvial phases had affected the humid tropics, continually modifying the vegetation cover and rates of surface erosion. The pattern of Quaternary climatic change in the tropics followed more or less the same pattern everywhere. There is evidence for an onset of late Pleistocene cooling by 40,000 B.P., and cool moist climates probably prevailed widely after 26,000/25,000 B.P., but the impact of full glacial conditions on tropical climates is most apparent between 22,000/20,000 B.P. and 14,000/12,000 B.P., when widespread cooling and drying of climates is recorded from both mountain and lowland environments. Coolest and driest conditions attach to a period during and following the last glacial maximum centered at 18,000 B.P. The rapid change towards post-glacial conditions may have begun before 13,000 B.P. and was certainly evident by 12,500 B.P. at most recorded sites. There followed everywhere a short but significant return to cooler and dryer conditions during the Younger Dryas Cold event, 11,000-10,000 B.P., after which conditions favouring a return to rainforest in the humid tropics were established by 9,000 B.P., when inter tropical lake levels were also high once more.

A tentative chronology of the late Quaternary environmental change based on evidence from all over the world is provided by M.F. Thomas in his book *Geomorphology in the Tropics-A study of Weathering and Denudation in Low Latitudes* 1994 (Thomas 1994: 204).

Degrees of aridity during the last glacial maximum differed from place to place but it occurred worldwide as the evidences say.

Evidence from Southeast Asia also presents a similar picture. In western Kalimantan, Indonesia (Latitude 0°, equatorial, 3200-5000 mm year) there are large accumulations of Pleistocene alluvial sediments, deposited in the coastal plains, which fall into at least two groups: an older terrace containing abundant timbers dated >40 000 B.P. at 6-12 m dept, and younger floodplain sediments for which there are two near basal dates of 10,500 B.P. The older suite is intriguing and it is interesting that similar dates have come from the 'old alluvium' in a coastal site in Perak, Malaysia. The sediments may relate to prolonged late Pleistocene low sea levels combined with drier levels. On the Indian Ocean marine oxygen-isotope record there are clear peaks at 85,000 B.P., 58,000 B.P. and 40,000 B.P., all possibly relevant to the formation of Older Alluvium of Southeast Asia. It is sufficient here to point out that the large accumulation of sediment in Kalimantan appear to have been deposited as a result of rapid erosion in small catchments, presently in an equatorial environment. Sudden floods, and rapid deposition appear to have been the conditions of sedimentation, and whilst neotectonic movements in this area cannot be ruled out (Thomas1994: 203, 233).

Around three hundred samples and an estimated 125,000 pollen grains collected from northeast Thailand especially from Lake Kumphawapi in the Banchiang province revealed a striking pattern of vegetation in the area during the Quaternary. Prior to the height of the last glacial period (20-40,000 years ago), forests in northeast Thailand was dominated by pine and oak instead of the modern tropical deciduous forests. As the global climate became cooler and drier at the height of the glacial period (around 18,000 years ago), conditions became so dry in northeast Thailand that many swamps and lakes dried out. As a result plant fossils that normally preserve in these wet environments were destroyed and no fossil information was recovered on the vegetation of the time. However, when conditions began to improve Lake Kumphawapi began to fill, and the plant fossils that were preserved in the lake sediments from this time indicate that the vegetation surrounding the lake had changed markedly. Due to increase monsoon rainfall during that early part of the Holocene epoch (10-6000 years ago), these forests were more diverse than their predecessors, and had clear similarities with modern Thai forests. Yet around 6500 years ago, something remarkable happened to the burgeoning forest of northeast Thailand. Many tree species decreased in abundance, while others disappeared from pollen records altogether. This striking forest decline is coincident with a substantial increase in the amount of microscopic charcoal particles preserved in the lake mud, a crude indication of fire in the lake catchment. The regional climate at the time of this episode was wet and warm relative to modern conditions, and there is no evidence to indicate a sudden change in climate to drier conditions that would promote natural burning. It might reflect the activities of prehistoric human populations (Penny 1999: 34-36).

Thus, in southeast Asia too like the rest of the world climatic fluctuations have occurred during the Quaternary and the last glacial maxima (18,000 B.P.) aridity was so severe that it has left behind distinct marks on the landscape in the form of thick alluvial deposits, low level lake deposits with pollens which clearly indicate the type of climate prevailing during the time of deposition.

Evidences of Quaternary climatic fluctuation and the last glacial maxima aridity have also come from the Indian subcontinent. Development of a distinct palaeosol over loess in Kashmir indicates climatic amelioration at 17,000-18,000 B.P. The southeastern monsoons seems to have weakened during this time while the northeastern monsoons seems to have strengthened. (Agrawal et al. 1990). The pre-13,000 B.P. sediments from the Didwana salt lake profile of Rajasthan reveal hypersaline conditions and a dune-building phase. Palynological studies carried out from other areas of Rajasthan also indicate hyperarid conditions prior to 10-000 B.P. (Singh et al. 1974).

Studies in upland western Maharashtra shows that most of the streams were aggrading during the last glacial period (21,000 to12,000 B.P.) and cutting/ eroding through the alluvial fills during the post glacial period (10,000 to 4,000 B.P.). Some evidence for aggradation is seen around 12,000 B.P. They showed that summer monsoons were weak during the terminal Pleistocene and were strong during the early-middle Holocene (particularly between 7,000 to 4000 B.P.). The late Pleistocene aridity in Maharashtra was severe (Mishra *et al.* 1998: 324). Available radiocarbon dates from the area shows that the gravel units within the late Pleistocene alluvium belong to the most arid phases of this period. At both Nevasa and Sangamner, gravel's with microliths date to 12,800 B.P. Dates of 10,000 B.P. from Asla, in the Krishna basin, 10,000 B.P. from Ghargaon in the Mula basin and 11,700 B.P. from Inamgaon in the Ghod basin probably date to the same aggradational episode. This dry episode may relate to the Younger Dryas event, which dates to 10,000 to11,000 B.P. At Nevis shells in the gravel date back to 16,400 B.P. (Sadakata *et al.* 1995: 43-44).

Studies made on microfossil evidence for changing salinity patterns in the Bay of Bengal over the last 20,000 years suggest reduced precipitation and river run-off in the northern Bay of Bengal during the last glacial interval (~18000 B.P.) and increased precipitation and run-off in the north, with possible increase in the strength of the southwest monsoon current south of 10° N during the MT interval (~10 500-12 500 B.P.). During the last glacial maximum (LGM) the salinity pattern probably results from decreased precipitation and decreased run-off by the Ganges- Brahmaputra and Irraway river systems, the main rivers which debauch into the Bay of Bengal. During the mid-termination (MT), the middle of the transition from glacial to interglacial global climatic regimes, salinity in the northern Bay of Bengal is caused by increased precipitation and run-off rather than by the influx of glacial melt water. These patterns can be correlated with faunal evidence from the western Arabian Sea that suggest decreased upwelling during the LGM and increased upwelling during the MT. This coupling of events may be associated with changes in the pattern of

intensity of circulation during the Southwest Monsoon: decreased intensity at the LGM (~1800 B.P.), and increased intensity at the MT (~10,500 to 12,500 B.P.).

This study was made by examining a transect of piston cores, seven in total at ~ 90° E from the equator into the Bay of Bengal. The stratigraphy of the transect is controlled by oxygen isotope profiles that are similar to the generalised patterns observed in other areas over the past 20,000 years. Significant foraminiferal variation has occurred in the Bay of Bengal over the last Ice-Age cycle. Because differential dissolution alters the ecologically related faunal composition of deep-sea sediments, two independent approaches were used to minimise the effects of dissolution: analysis of faunal changes within the resistant species population and application of dissolution-buffered palaeo-ecological transfer functions. Analysis of relative changes within the dissolution- resistant species population, dominated by *G. Duterei, G. Menardii, P. Obliquiloculata,* reveals the details of systematic palaeoecologic change down-core and along the transect and minimises faunal variation associated with differential dissolution. Most variation within the resistant population occurs in the northern Bay of Bengal with the degree of variation lessening to the south. Most change is seen in the salinity-sensitive species of *G. Dutertrei.* Comparison with the modern-day resistant population and associated surface water conditions reveals that during the LGM interval surface salinity in the Bay of Bengal were generally higher then today, especially in the north, while during the MT interval decreased salinity are indicated. These results also tally with the preliminary oxygen isotope results (Cullen 1981: 315-353).

This evidence confirms that during the last glaciation eastern and northeastern part of India including Myanmar experienced a much drier climate in comparison to the present. Rainfall was less and as a result the rivers were discharging much less water into the sea which had increased the salinity gradient.

Calcrete formation of pedogenic origin proved to have formed more or less contemporaneously with a microlith bearing colluvial horizon, in the Tarafeni valley of West Bengal, indicates that during the formation of this horizon the annual precipitation level in the area was between 400 mm to 600 mm. Fluorine/Phosphate dates obtained from bone samples collected from this horizon suggest a time period of Terminal Pleistocene (Basak *et al.* 1998: 732-740).

Palynological studies carried out in the Mirik Lake, Darjeeling, West Bengal (Sharma and Chauhan 1994) for recording the palaeovegetational history of the area gives an absolute date of 17,900 ± 600 B.P. for a regime which had open grassland. Thus, the last glacial maximum with open grassland and such grasses and sedges with other prominent herbaceous constituents agree well with a cool and dry climate. A pollen diagram constructed reveals that in the period between 18,000 and 12,000 B.P. this was replaced by oakpine forest, thus affecting a change from cool and dry to a warm climate. Around 11,000 B.P. there was again a deterioration of climate with a sudden increase in grasses and decline in oak. A climatic optimum was reached between 10 000 and 4 000 years B.P. with reintroduction of oak forest regime (Basak 1994: 72).

Palynological, microfaunal and sedimentological studies carried out in the south Bengal basin show that even the coastal parts of these humid to sub-humid regions faced the onslaught of environmental variations during the terminal Pleistocene. The occurrence of mangroves (which are sensitive to sea-level changes) at Digha, Kolaghat and Diamond harbour at elevations of –23 m, -21 m and –24 m during the 32,000 B.P., 22,000 B.P. and 14,460 B.P. agrees well with the global sea levels which were about 125 m, 55 m and 120 m below the present sea levels during the relevant times. The pre-Holocene mangrove swamps have been overlain by the microfaunal foraminifera that indicate the transgression of sea during this period. The presence of calcrete in these 30-50 m deep deltaic sediments suggest an arid phase (Basak 1994: 72).

Quaternary sediments of northeastern India constitute nearly one-third of the entire spread of the Quaternaries of the Indian sub-continent. The data revealed that the surficial deposits are formed under various depositional environments a) fluvial deposits occupying the Brahmaputra valley, intermontane valleys of Tripura, piedmont deposits flanking the Arunachal Siwaliks, narrow valley of Bomdila and Jayrampur; b) the glacial and glacio-fluvial-lacustrine deposits in Ziro valley, Arunachal Pradesh and c) lacustrine deposits of Loktak lake, Manipur. Mapping of these sediments has led to a four or five fold classification of the unconsolidated sediments. Out of which the two basal older units are highly oxidised and partly consolidated, and are assigned to the Pleistocene age. The upper two younger units are slightly oxidised and unconsolidated and are assigned to the Holocene age, based on morphostratigraphic, litho-pedologic criteria, and palynological remains corroborated by radiometric dating. A few intermontane basins and some isolated basins developed contemporaneously with the formation of the Brahmaputra basin during the post-Siwalik Himalayan orogenic movement. Its development is linked with the phases of uplift, glaciation and erosion of the Himalayas and basement tectonics affecting the Shillong massif and basin of deposition. The intermontane valleys flanked by north-south trending folded ridges are filled with well-developed Quaternary sediments, which cover over 40% area of the state. The upper Pleistocene terrace deposits, which overlie the dipping folded sequence of shale-siltstone, are highly oxidised into latosol and ferricretes at places. The upper part of the oldest terrace unit in Tripura is dated at 35,690 ± 3,050 B.P., by C-14 method. Sand plugs/ dykes of various dimensions profusely intrude the oldest terrace (T1) formation of Tripura. This emplacement shows anomalous concentration of caliche nodules, which indicate the prevalence of semi-arid conditions during the Upper Pleistocene. In the Brahmaputra and adjoining valleys in parts of Assam, Arunachal Pradesh and

Meghalaya fringes, generally four terraces have been mapped. The fluvial terrace deposit (T1) at Tipang, which is dissected, oxidised, orange to dark brown in colour, mapped in the south-eastern corner of Assam, along Tipang *nala*, at Singra in Lakhimpur district (north bank of Brahmaputra) and Barak Valley (North Cachar Hills district), have given radio carbon dates of 38,020 ± 2,230 B.P, 32,540 ± 130 B.P. and 40,000 B.P respectively. The fluvio-glacial deposits of the Ziro valley in Arunachal Pradesh indicated 40,000 B.P, while the oldest terrace deposits of the Khowai and Hoara valleys in Tripura date 35,690 ± 3,050 B.P. Further, the lacustrine deposits of Tale valley, Arunachal Pradesh and Lokatak lake deposits in Manipur gave consistent dates of 26,140 ± 780 B.P and 25,465 ± 660 B.P respectively. Thus, the radiocarbon dates of these formations though geographically separated and diverse in origin are fairly comparable. Therefore, these formations are coeval and placed in the upper Pleistocene. The younger terrace deposits, which are extensively developed at lower levels at valley flats, close to and related to the present day drainage system show negligible pedogenic and weathering profile and are greyish to yellowish in colour.

These deposits mapped in Upper Assam, Bomdilla, foot hills of Arunachal Pradesh in the Brahmaputra valley; fringe areas of Meghalaya, Goalpara and Kamrup Districts in the lower Brahmaputra valley, Assam and Khowai and Hoara Valleys in West Tripura district; as also unaltered sediments of Loktak Lake bed sequence in Manipur are correlatable and are accordingly placed in the Holocene. A comparative study of data available from the Brahmaputra basin, Arakan Youma basin and small, isolated basins in the lesser Himalayas brings out that these sediments belong to two distinct ages namely, Pleistocene and Holocene. The older shows varying degree of oxidation, while the later are unoxidised. The sediments of the Pleistocene in the Brahmaputra belong to three sub-cycles, each separated by a period of erosion leaving wide benches (terraces) on either side of the Brahmaputra valley. There is no data to indicate a lower age limit for the initiation of sedimentation in the Brahmaputra basin. There appears to be an appreciable break between sedimentation cycles of the Pleistocene and Holocene in all the basins, as the sediments of the later are unoxidised. The break in sedimentation may be related to global cooling due to glacial maximum (18,000 B.P.), resulting in cessation of sedimentation. The effects of this change in climate are also reflected in lowering of the sea level and impounding of water over the terrace.

The regional climatic scenario during the Pleistocene seems to be clear with convincing evidences from eastern India and Southeast Asia particularly. The last glacial maximum (LGM) heralded a period of cool, dry climate which brought a notable change of vegetation and landforms in this region which has been confirmed by palynological and palaeontological data. The present day wet tropical humid climatic areas of the world experienced semi-arid environment during the LGM and as the Holocene approached precipitation increased. Thus, a similar situation must have prevailed in Garo hills. A semi-arid environment is generally characterised by excessive soil stripping and seasonal rainfall after long dry spells. This excessive soil stripping from the Tura and Arbella range of mountains must have filled the subsided Ganol- Rongram river basin to an extent. Also during the heavy seasonal rainfall the rivers and streams erode the catchment areas and the drainage is heavily loaded with sediments. Once the rains recede the river loses its capacity to carry the load. As a result of this at times the channel gets blocked, as the sediments are not carried down. This choking of the drainage can create alluvial mounds similar to the once present in the study area. Similar features have been reported from the Kalimantan area of Indonesia.

Both these factors were aided by the fracture-controlled drainage of the region (Fig. 5). Just at Rongram, only 4 kms upstream of the confluence of the Ganol and the Rongram rivers there is a fault. This is a fracture or a zone of fractures along which there has been displacement of the sides relative to one another. This fault extends for almost 5 kms north-south interrupting the flow of both Ganol river and its tributary the Rongram river which flows westward from the south and southeastern corner of the study area respectively. The Pleistocene sediments were obstructed from flowing downstream and it might have also triggered a ponding environment. But these faults were no more active during the Holocene. Thus the rivers were actively eroding, cutting through the sediments and depositing further downstream. As noted earlier on the basis of physical characteristics this sediment in the study area can be divided into two stratigraphic units.

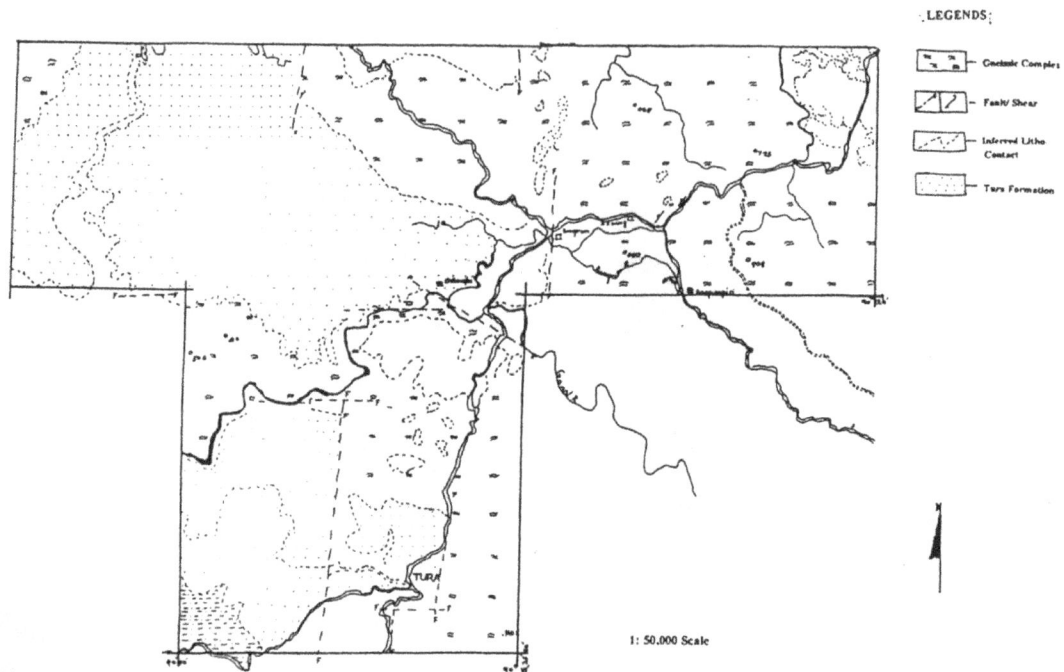

Figure 5: Geological Map Showing Faults

Plate 4: Colluvial Silt at Ida Bichik

The first or the lower unit (Unit1) is composed of strong brown highly oxidized alluvium (Plate 4) and the second unit is composed of yellowish brown slightly oxidized alluvium (Plate 5). On this basis it can be inferred that the time periods of the formation of these units is different. There appears to be an appreciable break in between sedimentation. Alluvium is a general term for clay, silt, sand, gravel, or similar unconsolidated detrital material deposited by a stream or other body of running water as sorted or semi-sorted sediment in the bed of the stream or on its flood plain or delta, or as a cone or fan at the base of a mountain slope. The break in sedimentation inferred on the basis of the rate of oxidization has been reported from other areas of Northeast India. In these areas C-14 dates have been obtained from these two units, which confirm that Unit 1 is Pleistocene in origin while Unit2 is of the Holocene period. The physical characteristics of both the units from the study area are similar to the dated units from other parts of Northeast India. Thus, they

24

seem to be the product of regional palaeoclimatic conditions of the area.

Plate 5: Yellowish Brown Alluvium

Also field observations have revealed that in the study area at Rongram, which is at 480 msl the division between the two units can be clearly marked. But as we proceed further upstream above 550 msl the size of Unit 1 gradually thickens and the Unit 2 is almost absent. But downstream of Rongram the size of the Unit 2 increases. So, it appears that in the upper course of the Ganol River and its tributary, the Rongram deposition mainly occurred during the Pleistocene as a result of crustal movement. These crustal movements the result of Himalayan orogeny 4 stopped in the Middle Pleistocene. Authors of the stone age industries which have been recovered from Unit1 inhabited these Pleistocene alluvial deposits. Highly oxidized similar sediments again bury these industries. Global cooling during the last glacial maxima (18,000 B.P) resulted in drier climatic conditions which triggered excessive soil stripping. So, deposition continued even after human occupation. Once Holocene started and precipitation increased the rivers were only eroding the sediments from the upper and middle courses and depositing them further downstream. The yellowish brown sediment seen approximately beyond 550 msl is better sorted and much finer. Lithic tools are also found in these Units. People lived on the Holocene deposit, which were again capped by similar sediments and a thick humus layer. Beyond Rongram the river basin gradually widens and comes out of the subsiding basin and flows on a flat surface. The fault was no more active during the Holocene. So, the down flow of the river was not interrupted and deposition is still occurring further downstream. In the study area the two main rivers are flowing on the bedrock. Deposition by a few first order streams in the study area is still continuing. These streams are eroding their catchment areas during the rainy season. These deposits are about a meter thick from which no cultural material of archaeological importance has been recovered.

Thus, it can be stated that this geomorphic unit which supported the Stone Age people and also the present day inhabitants has been formed as a result of:

(1) Crustal movements related with the morphotectonic upliftment of the Himalayan orogen, which simultaneously buckled up the pre-Cambrian massif of Meghalaya, triggering a phase of continental fluviatile sedimentation.
(2) Excessive soil stripping and heavy seasonal rainfall in response to semi-arid conditions prevailing during the last glacial maximum (LGM).

(3) Once precipitation increased with the onset of the Holocene, the rivers were eroding the catchment and cutting through the sediments and depositing them in the lower courses, which were also triggered by major eustatic changes. Massive valley filling is recorded.

Location of the sites clearly indicate that the settlers of the prehistoric period had chosen the area in between the Ganol and the Rongram river where the slope is comparatively gentle, for habitation. On the left bank of the Ganol river no site is recorded while on the right bank of the Rongram river only three sites are recorded. This selection made by the prehistoric inhabitants is noteworthy. The alluvial mounds in between the right bank of Ganol river and left bank of Rongram river was chosen specifically by the stone age people for habitation. The depressed trough or basin in between the Tura and Arbella ranges is enclosed in the three sides by steep slopes and dense vegetation. There is a narrow opening on the western side through which the rivers flow out of the basin. This enclosure provides a natural boundary that protects the basin from strong winds and heavy clouds that blow from the south, southwest and southeast and north and northeast. The luxuriant growth in the hill slopes is the home of a large number of edible plants and faunal species. Organic raw material like bamboo, cane and wood used as construction material and for making tools are found in abundance besides dolerite dyke material for making lithic tools. Also the slopes can be used for shifting cultivation. The alluvial terraces on which the lithic tools have been found is formed when a flood plain is abandoned through valley incision, thereby isolating the terrace surface from flooding. This provided a dry dwelling surface. Thus the chief factors behind the selection of the area by the Stone Age inhabitants are:

(I) Extreme fertility of the alluvium capable of supporting a very rich plant life, including edible foods and raw material for construction of shelter etc.

(II) Ample hunting ground and gathering area and cultivating fields.

(II) Presence of perennial sources of water.

(III) Availability of dolerite dyke exposures in the area and river pebbles making procurement of raw material for lithic tools an easy task.

(IV) Protection from bad weather and environmental hazards and defensibility.

(V) Dry ground surface to be used as dwellings.

THE ARCHAEOLOGICAL RECORD-SITES AND ARTIFACTS

Notion of site

An archaeological site is a place of past human activity generally indicated by a concentration of artifacts and discarded materials. The main aim of investigating a site is to understand the nature of the activities that took place there, and of the social groups that used it. The character of the sites depends on the nature of people who inhabit it and activities performed (Bahn and Renfrew 1993: 42, 170).

A site is usually the basic entity of archaeological analysis. The location and exploration of this unit is usually the goal of field research. Most sites in a traditional sense represent domestic or activity loci from which the exploitation of the surrounding environment took place (Dunnel and Dancey 1983: 271, 272). A site is also defined as a particular locale within a habitat, together with its immediate setting (Butzer 1983: 15). No society has ever lived, eaten, worked and died within the limits of a single site and consequently we cannot study society at this level alone. We have to study the surroundings to understand the type of resources available. The types of resources govern the different modes of adaptation developed by the inhabitants of an area. These modes of adaptation are the tool making techniques, type of tools produced, the subsistence and settlement pattern. The conceptual basis for understanding a region is that the archaeological record consists of systematically related artifacts across the landscape, peaking in intensity at particular locations usually designated as 'site' (Cherry *et al*. 1991: 21).

The archaeological record is believed to be spatially continuous and its structure may be described in terms of variable artifact density across the landscape. In this approach an individual site is not considered an independent entity but it is part of a whole larger complex, which is the region. The region is basically a geographic concept, which is an area bounded by topographic features such as mountains and bodies of water. An archaeological region may be defined as the area that contains a series of interrelated human communities sharing a cultural-ecological system (Sharer and Ashmore 1979: 76). This regional approach, pioneered by Lewis Binford (Binford: 1982) states that using *site* to structure recovery limits data collection to a small fraction of the total area occupied by any past cultural system. It systematically excludes nearly all evidences of the actual articulation between people and their environment. This bias in data collection can be minimised by adopting the landscape approach. Sites in this approach represent only a part of the total record, explicitly defined by density characteristic (Dunnel and Dancey 1983: 272). Points of variable artifact density have to be identified to understand human activity on the landscape. This can be done by undertaking site surveys.

In the site surveys areas with high artifact density are identified and plotted in a map and are treated as individual units. A combination of both the approaches will help us produce maps with points of variable artifact density plotted. A study of the relationship between the spatial distribution of artifacts and features on the landscape will help us to make inferences on the past use of the landscape. Through site surveys geographical and geological data can also be collected. This can provide clues for palaeoenvironmental reconstruction.

With the help of this data the type of resources available, the points where different resources occur, seasonal and perennial character of the resources can be assessed. Describing and interpreting the intensive activity areas, the off-site cultural residues and palaeoenvironmental data in the landscape helps in developing a holistic view of past human activities on the landscape (Zvelebil *et al*. 1992: 194-195). For this study a combination of site survey and landscape approach is adopted for recovering and interpreting the archaeological record of the Ganol-Rongram valleys.

Each occupation has its own spatial and temporal qualities, and each occupation leaves its own evidence of the nature of activities at this place in the form of artifacts, debris and features. In the Ganol-Rongram valleys besides the lithic artifacts and potsherds no other debris and features have survived which can help us to identify the different occupational activities. On the basis of typology and technology of the lithic tools and their stratigraphy the occupational sequences have to be identified.

The basic data recovery technique in the present study consisted of systematic surface collection directed towards producing distributions of artifacts within a carefully controlled space. An area with high artifact density is called a *site* and all other finds within a radius of one kilometre are identified as localities of that site in the study area.

As described in the previous chapter's the specific study area is formed by portions of the upper and middle course of the Ganol and Rongram which is approximately 200 sq km area. But some part within this limit could not be explored and in certain parts exploration was conducted but no cultural material was found. In the southern part of the study area from the source of the Ganol river to approximately seven kilometres downstream towards north the contour lines are very close and not contorted indicating steep slope. This area is covered with dense mixed jungle consisting of tropical evergreen forest and tropical moist deciduous forest. In the description of this forest in the previous chapter it has been stated that that the lush green vegetation forms a closed canopy making it impossible for light to penetrate. Structurally the forest displays zonation of trees with dense and impenetrable undergrowth. The dense humus and litter laden forest floor is often covered by grasses. Preservation of cultural material in a steep slope of this nature is a remote possibility. Also the type of forest cover makes visibility very poor. Due to these factors no exploration could be undertaken on these steep thickly vegetated slopes. Rongram River in the southeastern corner, till approximately five kilometres

downstream towards west the area have been explored under the present study but no cultural debris of past human activity was found. Here the contour lines are comparatively far apart indicating a gentle slope. But the prehistoric dwellers of the area seem to have avoided the areas in the immediate vicinity of the river for habitation. Majority of the sites are on the deposits created by first order and second order streams and at least 1 kilometre away from the main rivers. This choice must have been made to avoid the menace of frequent floodwaters during the rainy season, which rises to a level of approximately ten meters in the Ganol and Rongram rivers. The site are away from the rivers, mainly on the river terraces so that they may be free from the dangers of floods. Thus within the two hundred square kilometre area cultural material of the prehistoric inhabitants was recorded from a patch of approximately hundred square kilometres only.

In the Ganol- Rongram valleys there are surface sites, sub-surface sites and buried sites. These characteristic features of these categories will be dealt with under site description below. But it is noteworthy to mention that even though human habitation continues appreciable destruction of the sites has not taken place. Certain situations under which the sites in the area are preserved will be discussed after each site has been discussed in detail.

The few surface sites are on the bedrock. The bedrock is exposed at an altitude of 600 m msl at Missimagiri, which is a flat top tableland. Deposition is very thin on this surface on which lithic tools have been found. At Chitra Abri and Mokbol Bichik on the slope of the alluvial mound dolerite dyke exposures are very close to the bedrock. As dyke material was profusely used by the prehistoric settlers for making tools these are found littered on the bedrock surface with cores, flakes and chips. Rongram is a sub surface site. The top layers of the alluvial mound on which tools are found had been sliced down for the construction of an Inspection Bunglow exposing the implementiferous layer. Tools have been found in a half- buried condition at this site. Didami, Gawak Abri, Ida Bichik are fully buried sites. Various post-depositional processes act on the artifacts in these sites. On the basis of the state of preservation sites in this study are classified into three categories as follows:

Type 1: *In situ* sites, which were buried immediately or shortly after their abandonment and remain buried. The degree of patination on lithics is nil or limited in such sites and this is the main criteria for identifying sites of type1.

Type 2: *In situ* sites exposed by the removal of the overlain sediments without considerably disturbing the original arrangement of the tools.

Type 3: Locations with scattered artifacts on the surface. The original sedimentary context is unknown.

Sites will be described below depending on which type they belong to. Under type1 there are two sites Gawak Abri and Didami. Rongram IB, Ida Bichik, Bibragiri, Missimagiri, Selbal Bichik, Mokbol Bichik II, are sites under type 2. The two other sites, namely Chitra Abri, Mokbol Bichik I fall under type 3. From Rongram IB, Gawak Abri, Ida Bichik and Didami samples of the alluvium and colluvium were collected. These samples collected from specific depths were chemically analysed. The type of analysis undertaken consisted of Calcium Carbonate determination by Rapid Tritation method (after Piper 1978), Organic Carbon determination was done by Colorimetric method, PH determination by BDH indicator papers and the soil colour was classified according to the Munsell Soil colour chart. Mechanical analysis of the samples was undertaken by Pipette method for identifying the type of sediments that constitute the alluvium and colluvium and their individual percentages. The results of these various tests are used in the interpretations below.

Site Description

i) **Gawak Abri**- It is located approximately 8 km downstream from the source of the river Rongram. The river Rongram flows one and a half kilometer away to the west of the site. On its southeastern side less then half km away is the Selbal stream, a first-order channel of the river Rongram and on its southern side is the Ida stream, a second order stream of the same river system. The altitude is approximately 550 m msl and the area is 3 sq km. Artifacts were recovered from the northern side of the mound.

The deposit within which the tools are found is almost six meters in thickness on the Southern side of the mound while on the northern side it is about four meters in thickness. The implementiferous layer is overlain by a deposit of 1 and 1/2 m on the northern side of the mound. The alluvium is strong brown in colour. There is a slight difference in shade between the alluvium above 47 cm and the alluvium below it. The former is 7.4 Yr, 5/8 while the later is 7.5 Yr 4/6. Sedimentological analysis of the deposit has revealed that above 47 cm the percentage of clay is much more than the lower levels while the percentage of total silt also is comparatively higher. But the percentage of sand both coarse and fine is very high in the bottom layers. In 20 gms of sediment the percentage of sand was 68.85%. The rest of the sediments consisted of silt of which coarse silt was 26.7%. In the upper levels also percentage of coarse silt was similar. This indicates that the material is coarse and not well sorted. Percentage of clay is negligible in the whole deposit and the percentage of medium and fine silt is also very low. The coarse sand particles and the quartz gravels separated by dry sieving are very angular. This indicates that the material has not been transported from a very long distance. The alluvium is acidic and the organic carbon content is high. Dolerite dyke exposures are present in the southern and south-western corner of the site.

The total thickness of the implementiferous layer is almost one meter. Cultural material collected from the site consisted of lithic tools and pottery. A total number of 123 lithic artifacts and 50 potsherds were collected from a 2/2 m trial trench. It can be called a single culture site on the basis of the typological character of the tools. The lithic assemblage consisted of ground and polished celts, short axes, chipped celts, and a very high percentage of micro size flakes, some of which were probably used. A thin patina is seen on the surface of the tools. The flake scars are sharp and fresh. The pottery consisted of two varieties classified on the basis of colour and fabric. One was very coarse black colour pottery and the other was also of coarse variety but comparatively finer with a thin grey slip. Very few rim sherds were recovered for reconstructing the shapes.

ii) **Didami**- This site is located at a distance of seven km towards north, from the source of river Ganol. It is at an altitude of 916 m msl. It is on the bank of a first order stream called Didami Biphek which joins the Didami Chiring, a tributary of Ganol. The Ganol flows at a distance of about two and a half km on the south-western side of the site.

An exposed section on the eastern side of the mound was studied. This section is very close to the stream Didami Biphek, which flows on the eastern boundary on the bedrock. All other secondary and tertiary lithostratigraphic units are unexposed. The pebbly horizon identified in the region as Tertiary- Quaternary boundary is partially exposed. On it the Quaternary alluvial deposit is seven meters thick. The implementiferous layer is approximately two meters thick. It sits on a meter thick deposit and is buried by three and half meter deposit. The eastern section is exposed for almost half a kilometre but the implemetifeorus layer is not visible all along the section. The horizontal extent of the tool-bearing layer is approximately 3m. 65-70% of the alluvium consists of sand. Rest is silt while the percentage of clay is negligible. Dolerite dykes in a half-buried state are noticed on the eastern side of the mound.

The lithic assemblage solely consists of bifacially flaked artifacts, blade flakes and probably utilised flakes. Seventy five lithic artifacts were collected from the exposed two meter section. Patination is almost absent and the flake scars are sharp and fresh. One discoidal core was recovered from the site.

The total extent of the site could not be ascertained as the area is thickly vegetated. On the surface of the mound no tools were found. The deposit on the western side of the mound is even thicker. An approximately two meter vertical section exposed on the western side of the mound revealed no cultural material. In the study area the altitude of this site is the highest.

iii) **Rongram I B** (Plate 6): The river Rongram flows through a relatively flat and narrow basin for a distance of about eight kilometre upstream from its confluence with the Ganol river. The Rongram IB site is located four kilometre upstream from the confluence on the eastern bank of the river. Occurring at an altitude of 458 m msl it is the remnant of an ancient terrace. The approximate height of the mound from the present river bed is10 m. The mound measures 39 m x 27 m in size.

Plate 6: Rongram IB Terrace Section at Rongram IB site

The geological history of the Ganol-Rongram valleys is well preserved and visible in the exposed section of the mound. The floor of the mound is formed by Archaean Gneissic rock. Over the Archaeans rest some Gondwana conglomerates. Sediments of the Tertiary age form the next layer. This is the Tura sandstone. A pebbly horizon composed of sand, clay, pebbles and gravel sits on the Tura sandstone. In the north-western, northern and northeastern section of the mound this layer is highly ferricretised and compact. But in the southern corner it is non-ferricretised and loose. This is the Tertiary-Quaternary boundary. This layer is capped by alluvium, approximately 1m thick. It is of two distinct varieties identified on the basis of colour. From the surface to 36 cms. the colour of the alluvium is dark yellowish brown (10YR: 4/6, according to Munsell colour chart) and below it is strong brown coloured (7.5YR:

5/6, according to Munsell colour chart). The dark yellowish brown alluvium consists of 50% sand and almost an equal percentage of silt. Of this coarse silt amounts to 27.82%. Fine silt and clay are very less. In the strong brown coloured alluvium percentage of sand is even higher. It is above 65% of which fine sand is 36.86%. Total silt amounts to 30.65% of which 22.27% is coarse silt. On the basis of the angularity of the sand particles and gravel separated by dry sieving it can be stated that the sediments have not been transported from a very long distance. In the study area the altitude of this site is the lowest and the site lies at the farthest distance from the source of both the Ganol and Rongram rivers. The source of the Rongram is at a distance of 15km southeast of the site.

Chemical analysis of the alluvium revealed that both the yellowish brown and strong brown alluvium is acidic. Calcium carbonate is absent while the content of organic carbon is medium. This evidence indicates high rainfall, humidity and thick vegetation in the area when the alluvium was deposited. But this data is insufficient for drawing conclusions on the past ecological condition of the area.

The surface layer is implementiferous. Ground Neolithic celts were found in a half-buried condition. Till 36 cm below surface ground and polished celts, pestles and a few flakes were found. Below this level prolific occurrence of edge-ground tools, chipped tools, short axes and pebble scrapers and choppers is noteworthy. At 55 cm level flattish stones with average length and breadth of 16 cm and 15 cm respectively were uncovered. These could have been used as grinding stones. Considering the fact that they occur in one particular horizon in a cluster it can be inferred that they were part of a rammed floor. The implementiferous layer continues till 67 cm. The reddish brown alluvial layer continues for another 50 cm below surface. This can be called the virgin layer. On the basis of tool typology and stratigraphy this site can be called a multicultural site. Sixty seven lithic artifacts were recovered from a 2/3m trial trench taken at the south-western corner of the site. A considerable portion of the alluvial deposit has been sliced down for the construction of an Inspection Bungalow of the Public Works Department exposing the implementiferous layer. On the basis of the height of an adjacent intact alluvial mound on the western bank of the river it can be said that the original height of the alluvial deposit of the Rongram IB site must have been approximately 10 m. Of this approximately 2 m deposit is still intact.

iv) **Ida Bichik**: This site, as is true of most of the other sites, gets its name from a second order stream called the Ida Chiring. This stream joins the Selbal, a first-order stream of the Rongram river. The Ida Chiring has a course of one and a half kilometres and it forms the northern boundary of the site. The northern, western and southern boundaries of the site are formed by the Ida chiring and on its eastern boundary is the Ida Biphek, a third-order stream. The site is at an altitude of 550 m msl. On the eastern boundary there is a dolerite dyke across the Ida Biphek stream.

All the streams here flow on the bedrock. The pebbly horizon is visible on the southern side of the mound and no other lithostratigraphic units are visible. This horizon is approximately 2m thick above the bedrock and the alluvial deposit is approximately 6m thick. The size of the mound is 1 sq km. The colour of the alluvium is Strong Brown (7.5 YR 4/6-Munsell colour chart) and it is acidic. Approximately 65% of sand is recorded from a 20gm sample of which 37.18% is fine sand. Silt content is 34% of which coarse silt constitutes 14.73%. This sample was collected from a depth of 2 m from the surface.

Lithic tools were found in a half-buried condition on the southern side of the mound that had been cleared for cultivation and a part of it was sliced down to make a pathway across the mound. One hundred artifacts were collected. Surface exploration of the mound did not yield any tools. The implementiferous layer is sealed by deposits measuring 2 to 2 ½ m in thickness. The thickness of the implementiferous layer could not be ascertained. Ground and polished celts, chipped celts, varieties of flake tools like points, scrapers, flake blanks, pebble cores were collected from the site. Almost 60% of the assemblage constitute of ground and chipped celts. A pebble core measuring 25cm x15cm x 15cm in size was found. Thus, river pebbles were also used to make tools besides dyke material.

Just half a kilometre on the southeastern corner of this site across the Ida Biphek there is another tool scatter which is exposed on the surface. This mound has been extensively used for cultivation and a part of the mound has been dug and flattened. On this surface tools are exposed. On the basis of distance this is considered as a locality of Ida Bichik and is named Ida Bichik II. The tool assemblage is similar to Ida Bichik I and the density of tools is also almost similar. No collection was made from this locality. The size of this mound .75 sq km.

v) **Bibragiri**: It is located on the eastern bank of the Ganol river, eleven kilometre downstream at an altitude of approximately 800m msl. On its western boundary is a deep gorge at the bottom of which the Ganol flows on the bedrock. The site consist of a cluster of three alluvial mounds interspersed with dolerite dykes. The height of the alluvium in all the three mounds is different. The ferricretised pebbly horizon is exposed in the north-eastern mound, on which there is a five meter thick alluvial deposit. Just behind it less then half a kilometre on the south-western corner there is another mound with approximately fifteen meter of alluvium. No other lithostratigraphic units are exposed. The alluvium is strong brown in colour with a very high percentage of quartz angular gravel. Through surface exploration presence of lithic tools on these two mounds have been confirmed. No tools were found on the third mound in the south-eastern corner.

The northeastern mound in this study will be referred as Bibragiri I and the south-western mound will be referred as Bibragiri II. Almost three meter deposit in Bibragiri I was sliced down and the surface levelled for constructing a soil conservation department office. At Bibragiri II an orange orchard was started on an experimental basis and pits were dug for planting the saplings. In the process the surface layer was considerably disturbed and the implementiferous layer was exposed. Pathways were constructed criss crossing the mound at different levels exposing the implementiferous layer at various depths. On this basis it is ascertained that the implementiferous layer at Bibragiri II is more then two meter thick.

At Bibragiri I pebble short axes, large and medium size flake tools constitute the assemblage. At Bibragiri II short axes only occur sporadically. Blade flakes dominate the assemblage. Fifty and 150 lithic artifacts were studied from Bibragiri I and II respectively from a 2x3m grid at Bibragiri I and 5x3m grid at Bibragiri II.

vi) **Missimagiri** (Plate 7): This site located at an altitude of 750 m msl gets its name from a stream called Missima, a tributary of Ganol river. It is thirteen kilometre downstream of Ganol on its eastern bank. The Archaean gneissic bedrock is exposed at this altitude and patches of Gondwana conglomerate and Tertiary sandstone are also seen. Due to these exposures a considerably flat surface occurs at this altitude forming a tableland. Deposition is very thin on this surface. Huge dykes of dolerite are seen in and around the site. At the northern boundary of the present habitation area a 2 m thick deposit consisting of a gritty, strong brown alluvium is present. In extent this layer is half a square kilometre, which dips down slope in the northern direction. Part of it was sliced down for constructing a house of the village headman in 1976. The implementiferous layer was exposed in the process.

Plate 7: Northeastern Side of Missimagiri Site with exposed Dolerite Dykes

The north-south extension of the site is 145 m and the east-west extension is 100 m. Tools were found in fully buried and half buried condition. Blade flakes their size ranging from 2 cm to 10 cm dominates the assemblage. Roughly cylindrical cores are found in considerable number. In a grid of 2x2 m seven such cores were recorded.

This site is one of the richest sites of the area. In comparison to the site area the tool density is very high. Easily available raw material in the form of the dolerite dykes and the flat hard bed rock surface provided a very convenient place for stone tool making. An inventory of artifacts collected from the site by a previous worker is reproduced below for a better understanding of the character of the site.

Types of artifact collected Number Percentage
1. Cores 73 2.90
2. Cleaver type flakes 48 1.91
3. Scrapers 242 9.64
4. Blades 316 12.58
5. Simple flake 596 23.83
6. Levallois Flake 56 2.23
7. Knife 50 1.99
8. Points 74 2.94
9. Borer 32 1.27
10. Arrowhead 30 1.19
11. Spearhead(leaf points) 16 0.63
12. Notched flake 26 1.03
13. Waste flakes and chips 300 11.95
14. Diverse Group 501 19.96

Total 2501
(Reproduced from Sonowal, Minarva 1987: 52)

The presence of an appreciable number of cores (72), unmodified simple flakes (596) and debitage clearly indicated that this was a factory site. The size of the tools varied between 1cm to 15 cm. Core dimensions were equally varied.

vii) **Selbal Bichik**: At an altitude of 550 m msl this site is located on the eastern bank of the Selbalgiri stream, a first order stream of the Rongram river. It is at a distance of two kilometre towards south of the Tura-Williamnagar road. The foot path follows the channel of the river and this forms the western boundary of the mound.

At present the river flows on the bedrock and deposits sediments on the eastern bank. On the western bank no recent deposit is seen. The alluvial deposit on the mound is approximately 4 m in thickness. The surface layer is formed by a 75 cm thick humus layer. This layer sits on a yellowish brown silty layer below which is a strong brown layer. The sedimentological studies revealed that the composition of this alluvium is very much identical to the Rongram IB site. Length-wise the mound is 200 m and breadth-wise it is 100 m. Surface exploration undertaken under the present study yielded few tools. Only 25 artifacts were found on the surface. These two 2 ground and polished celts, 1 chipped celt, 2 hammer stones and 9 flakes. But still on the basis of previous reports (*IAR* 1965-66, 1969-70: 1) and collections made and reported by previous workers (Sharma 1966; Mahanta 1993) this site has been taken up for study. It is one of the most frequently visited site of the area and one of the oldest reported site.

viii) **Mokbol Bichik II** (Plate 8): This site is located north of the Missimagiri site at an altitude of 630 m msl. On its southern boundary is the Missima stream and on its northern boundary is the Mokbol Chiring, a second order stream which joins the Selbal stream. On both of its boundaries there are prominent dolerite dyke exposures. It is within 1 km radius of the Missimagiri site and also another site, the Mokbol Bichik. On the basis of the similarity of tools with the site of Mokbol Bichik it has been categorised as Mokbol Bichik II.

Plate 8: Mokbol Bichik II and Missimagiri

The size of the mound is half a square kilometre roughly. Tools are found in half buried condition on the surface of the site.

Below the humus layer the alluvium is strong brown. The total thickness of the implementiferous layer could not be measured as during the time of exploration the site was under cultivation. The total thickness of the alluvial layer is approximately 6 m.

Lithic tools found in the site are slightly larger then medium size tools and they are mostly made on slabs extracted from the dykes. Large size flakes, that were probably utilised were also collected. No systematic collection could be attempted as the mound was under cultivation. Sixty seven artifacts found within an area of 5x5 m approximately were studied. But horizontal and vertical displacement of the artifacts was noticed due to agricultural activity.

ix) **Citra Abri**: The site is located on a steep ridge at the left bank of the river Rongram, at a distance of about two kilometre on the southwest of Rengsangiri village, which is at a distance of five kilometre northeast of Rongram IB site. It is located at an altitude of 500m msl on the slope of the Arbella mountain. On the contour map this area is marked with closely clustered contour lines and not contorted. This indicates steep slopes, which at present are incessantly used by the inhabitants for shifting cultivation.

The site is exposed on the bedrock. Ground and polished Neolithic celts and flake artifacts constitute the assemblage. Double shouldered celts were found only in this site in the study area. An inventory of artifacts made on the site showed a high percentage of flakes (56%) in comparison to ground and polished tools. Fifty artifacts were studied from a 5x5 m grid. But in the absence of a clear stratigraphy it is hard to identify if the tools belong to the same context or they belong to two different contexts.

x) Mokbol Bichik I: This site gets its name from a second order stream, the Mokbol Chiring. This stream is about one and a half kilometre in length and flows from the east to the west ultimately joining the Selbal stream. At present it flows on the bedrock. At a distance of 300 km on the north there is a huge dolerite dyke exposure at the foot of an alluvial mound. The site can be called a surface site as the artifacts are exposed on the bedrock.

The tool assemblage mainly consists of tools made on slabs extracted from the dyke. Large size flakes, which were probably utilized are also found in considerable number. A few short axes and a huge chunk of waste flakes were the remaining type of artifacts. But as the original sedimentary context of the assemblage is unknown it is difficult to assess the time period of the assemblage. Eighty-two artifacts were collected from 5x5 m grid.

The Sedimentary Record of the Sites

The above site descriptions makes it clear that the sediments within which the lithic tools are found contain a very high percentage of coarse angular sand and silt. The probable geomorphological processes that resulted in the formation of these deposits have been described in chapter two. Sedimentological analysis of samples collected from three sites located at different altitudes reveal certain patterns. The sediments are of coarser variety. Gravels separated by dry sieving are angular which suggest that the sediments have not been transported from a long distance. Percentage of clay is negligible. The highest amount does not exceed 7%. At Rongram IB site and at Gawak Abri an upward fining sequence is noticed. Percentage of silt is comparatively more in the top layers (Rongram IB-42.53% and Gawak Abri-40.7%) while percentage of sand is very high at the lower levels (RongramIB-63.59% and Gawak Abri-68.84%). Silt (25% to 30%) is also present at Didami which is at an altitude of 916 m msl. It is clear that when these sediments were deposited the rivers had the capacity to drain out only the clay while all the other material like silt and sand was deposited. Analysis of sediments from recent river deposits in the area shows the presence of a high percentage (61.94%) of coarse sand. Thus, under the present climatic conditions deposition of the finer sediments is minimum (Plate 9).

Plate 9: Recent Deposits of the Selbal Chiring

From this we can postulate that climatic conditions different from the present prevailed during the period when these deposits were created. Deposition occurs when the river does not have the capacity to carry the material. Probably rainfall was lower than at present, so the rivers had less water or the drainage was obstructed. The reasons, cited in Chapter two, are dry climatic conditions during the late Pleistocene and the role of tectonics or cumulative affect of both these factors.

These sediments till date have been always defined as alluvium. But the sedimentary analysis clearly proves that the character of the sediments do not confirm to the textbook definition of alluvium. The angularity of the gravel within the sediment indicates that the material have not been transported from a long distance. The coarse character suggests that there has been no sorting of the material. In the samples below 550-600 m msl some amount of upward fining sequence is noticed but above it no such situation exists. Also it is difficult to perceive a situation when the rivers can climb up till the height above 600 m to 900 m msl when it did not have the capacity to carry down

the silt. It is much more convincing to accept these deposits as mass wasting, gravity or debri flow materials and products of soil creep from the Arbella and Tura mountain ranges. This can thus be called colluvial silt.

Colluvia includes coarse, unsorted talus and landslide or slump debris on steep slopes below cliffs, and texturally variable, bedded sediments mantling footslopes. The definition of colluvium embraces deposits transported by mass movement rather than sediments deposited by running water (Botha and Partridge 2000: 90). Such colluviation during the late Pleistocene have been reported recently from different parts of the world. Botha *et al.* (2000) has reported it from South Africa, Corvinus has reported it from Nepal and similar formations were observed in Thailand. In the northeastern region of India also such formations have been reported from Manipur. In the Imphal Valley these deposits, dating between 25-11 ka, disconformably cap fluvio-lacustrine formations (Thokchom 1987). From Garo Hills also Medhi reported terminal Pleistocene colluvial silts (1981) but the term alluvium prevailed within the scientific community for defining these deposits. Thus, though the term alluvium is used in this study initially to define these deposits it is proposed that for future studies these deposits should be referred as colluvial silts. The deposits below 550m msl can be called sandy silt or silty sand. Pure alluvium is present beyond the boundary of the study area which is the confluence of the Ganol and the Rongram. In the RongramIB site some amount of alluviation has occurred for which the yellowish brown younger alluvium and the strong brown older alluvium is distinctly visible. The percentage of Fine Sand, Silt and Clay when added is more then 70% at Rongram IB in both the layers. In geological science if addition of the percentage of Fine Sand, Silt and Clay in any deposit is more then 70% that deposit is classified as loess. This loessic character of the RongramIB sediments is intriguing. The count from Ida Bichik is 85.275% while at Gawak Abri 69.406% and 66.492% and at Didami 65.43% and 61.590% from Layer I and 2 respectively. These deposits are the result of some amount of fluvial activity, gravity or debris flow material deposits but it is difficult to envisage aeolian activity in the region. This high percentage of silt and fine sand is the result of loss of capacity by the rivers when these deposits were created. At present the rivers are depositing more then 60% coarse sand. All the finer material are drained out from the area and deposited further downstream. The Himalayan orogeny four was responsible for large scale denudation of the soil cover of the Tura Mountains which filled the valley. A phase of continental fluviatile sedimentation during the middle Pleistocene has been recorded in the Meghalaya plateau (Sinha *et al.* 1981-82: 39). These deposits probably were created during this event. There is no soil formation in the area which indicates that the landscape was dynamic. The deposition was episodic which continued till the present climatic situation set in around 10,000 B.P. Artifacts in the sites like Didami, Bibragiri, Missimagiri are found buried within these deposits.

The authors of the flake-blade assemblage, the bifaces and pebble tools settled on the Middle Pleistocene deposits during the late Pleistocene when the climate was much drier than at present. Denudation from the hills continued till the beginning of the Holocene. At the end of the Pleistocene when the rainfall increased the rivers started eroding these deposits resulting in the deposition of much finer sediments downstream at sites like Rongram IB. On these sediments the authors of the celt assemblage lived. That is why most of the earlier workers reported the sites with the celts as surface sites as deposition was very less after the rainfall increased and these sites were either surface or sub surface sites. The strong brown colour of the colluvial silt has formed as result of pedogenesis. This proves that it is older then the yellowish brown sandy silt within which the celts occur. Radiometric dates from different parts of Northeast India of this two layers (Ramesh 1999: 13-35) given in Chapter 2 confirms the middle-upper Pleistocene origin of the strong brown layer and Holocene origin of the yellowish brown layer.

Site Preservation

Traditional Garo villages consisted of closely clustered houses. The rest of the area was used for shifting cultivation. For this cultivation they never till and dig the soil and take precautionary measures to avoid erosion. Sites which have been reported thirty years ago are still found intact today (*IAR* 1966:2). Under the system of rotation of fields a patch of land is cultivated for maximum of two years and then it is abandoned for at least eight years today. In the past the period of abandonment was even longer. The vegetation soon rejuvenates. Rainfall is intercepted by taller plants, which break raindrop impact and prevent direct rain splash on mineral soil. Organic leaf litter on various of stages of decomposition covers the ground and creates a topsoil layer that cushions water impact, while also acting as sponge to soak it up. The microfauna of the organic topsoil also maintain a spongy soil structure by converting organic residues into beneficial byproducts, enhancing the aeration essential for good plant growth and allowing water to infiltrate the soil. This diverts surface water from rapid runoff. Meanwhile the rooting network helps bind the soil. The net result is that the impact of surface runoff is reduced, soil moisture is enhanced, and ground water seepage is maintained, even during drier times of the year. Stream discharge immediately after heavy storms is reduced or delayed, and dry season flow is sustained. This controls erosion even during the rainy season (Butzer 1992: 123). Ethnographic observation in the study area revealed that steep slopes prone to erosion are avoided for building dwelling structures. People tend to select small areas of flat land even on an undulating landscape. In this valley there are localities of long term geomorphic stability even though the closely clustered contour lines and the altitude indicate a mountainous terrain with dendritic drainage.

This valley has been never abandoned by people from the unknown earliest times when the first settlers inhabited the area till the present. Within the valley, which is some 50 km in breadth and almost the same size lengthwise depending on their priorities and necessities people change their point of residence and other activity areas. For instance, a piece of homestead land after a certain period of time is converted into an agricultural field. As the inhabitants are shifting cultivators at present rotation of cultivated plots is compulsory and people shift their points of residence as part of their cultural behaviour. In either way the land is used. Impressions left by the previous activities on the landscape often overlaps and part of it is erased. In the process we lose valuable contextual data. The stratigraphy of the area is quite clear. But there are distinctly different tool assemblages which occur within the same context. For example, at Chitra Abri ground and polished celts, which are agricultural tools found on the bed rock and at Mokbol Bichik I a flake tool assemblage which resembles a hunter-gatherer tool kit is also found at the bed rock. Typologically these two assemblages belong to two different cultural periods. But as their context of origin is same they confuse us. The same assemblages in the area are also found in a buried context. The exposure of the tools on the bed rock may be the result of erosion or may be the tool makers probably occupied the bed rock and made tools from the dolerite dykes which are very close to the bed rock in both the areas.

These bed rock exposures are also not always visible. When the vegetation is thick in the area it is completely buried by tree litter and weeds which grow on it. Only when the land is cleared for cultivation this cover is removed. It stays exposed at present time's maximum for two years and for another eight to six years they stay covered. The number of years they are covered was even longer in the past. Crops are planted during these two years all around the bedrock. When the plants grow it is covered partially. During the sowing and harvesting season it is used as sitting platform. This is the time when the tools are fully exposed. There is minor displacement of the tools for a few centimetres. Otherwise there are no other erosional forces like water from a flowing stream etc. which can cause major displacement. Also this bed rock exposures except at the site of Missimagiri is always at the foot of the mound. They form a flat surface and there is no scope of tools rolling

down. The locus of the surface site of Chitra Abri, first reported in 1957 is still the same today.

From the site description it is clear that in majority of the sites the implementiferous layer was exposed as a result of slicing of the top layers of the alluvial mounds or due to some other disturbance. On this basis it can be stated that these sites are all buried sites. But the thickness of the top layers removed is not recorded. The total height of the deposit becomes a matter of imagination. As a result the exact depth at which the implementiferous layer begins remains unknown. The amount and type of deposition that had occurred after the site had been abandoned by the settlers is lost. This data could have provided vital information on the climatic condition of the area and it has also adversely affected in establishing a relative chronology of the tool assemblages.

The vegetation in the area described in detail in the previous chapter reduces visibility of the sites. Impenetrable growth makes surface exploration a very hazardous and costly affair. Site visibility improves when a piece of land is cleared for cultivation by slash and burn method or for constructing a house etc. A well reported site Watri Abri within the study area could not be explored as almost six years back the site was abandoned after cultivation and at present it is covered with dense vegetation. But under this situation no erosional processes can harm the site and the site is well preserved. This is the main reason that sites, which were reported a decade earlier (*IAR* 1967: 2) are still found intact today. Another cluster of sites in the study area, at Ganolgiri has become completely inaccessible because almost ten years back after it was abandoned as an agricultural field for the vegetation to rejuvenate it was adopted by a herd of wild elephants as their shelter. At present it is a thick jungle and no human activity continues in the area. Preservation of sites under such circumstance is not known.

Fully buried sites like Gawak Abri, Didami, Bibragiri and Mokbol Bichik II are intact. But sites like Rongram IB have been partially destroyed by post-depositional processes. Artifacts found in half buried condition are heavily weathered. In certain cases the displacement on the surface has changed the context of the tools. For example at Rongram IB site we have tools of three typological varieties. Tools collected from the surface belong to two different typologies. One consist of ground and polished celts and the other is made of chipped celts, edge ground celts etc. But today both these assemblages are considered contemporary as they are found in the same context. This might be the true scenario but it might also be so that the ground and polished tools belong to a much younger industry succeeding the edge ground and chipped celts. Due to lack of preservation certain facts remain unclear.

Site Setting

The local habitat or site setting forms an integral part of the archaeological record. This area is exploited by the inhabitants for procuring food and other necessary raw materials. Thus, the type of resources available determines the way people behave on the landscape and the land use patterns.

The sites with the ground and polished agricultural tools are found in the area with gentle slopes and they are closely clustered. These sites are Rongram IB, Chitra Abri, Selbalgiri, Ida Bichik I and II and Gawak Abri. This agrees very well with the settlement pattern of the present-day inhabitants of the area. The Garos who are shifting cultivators live in villages in closely clustered houses. The fertile alluvial mounds around the area are used for cultivation. The cultivators prefer gentler slopes, a perennial source of water as the most convenient place for habitation. Together with this the stone age people cantered around dolerite dyke exposures, the prime source of raw material for making tools. The rocky steep slopes of the higher ridges are inconvenient as they are not as fertile as the alluvium. Deposition is very less in these slopes and if they are cleared of vegetation with the slightest disturbance due to rain or tectonics the deposits will roll down the slopes. The setting of the sites with the ground and polished agricultural tools match closely

with the settlement pattern of the present day cultivators of the area. The shifting cultivators of the area at present clear at least 1.5 sq km area for cultivation. A family of four to eight members can subsist for a year on the produce of this plot in present times. A village has to clear every year a certain amount of cultivable land depending on the necessity. If a village has twenty households they will at least need 30 sq km cultivable area. It might be slightly more or less. With homestead land and cultivable land a village has at least 40 to 50 square kilometre area under its disposal. This can be identified as the site territory. Around each Neolithic site in the valley a considerable amount of cultivable land is present. There is regular rotation of fields for which there must be some extra land available. According to the present cycle after six to eight years they again come back to the same plot. Earlier this gap was much longer. On the western and southern side of the Rongram IB site the alluvial deposits extends to a distance of about 20kms. These are terraces of the Rongram river. Stray finds are recorded on these terraces but no sites have been found. On this basis we can state that these terraces were used by the ground and polished tool-makers for shifting cultivation. The next site Chitra Abri is at a distance of 6 km to the southeast of Rongram IB site. It is the only site on the eastern bank of the Rongram river at the foothills of the Arbella mountain. Cultivation was possible at the foothills of the Arbella mountain with much gentler slopes. These slopes formed the eastern boundary of the site. In the southern and northern side the alluvial deposits extend up to a considerable distance providing ample land for shifting cultivation. Ida Bichik is at a distance of about 4 km in the southwest of Chitra Abri. Around this area there is a cluster of sites which include Ida Bichik I and II, Gawak Abri, Selbal Bichik which give the impression of a village with closely clustered houses. On the southern and western sides of this cluster the sandy silt deposits are very thick and extend up to a considerable distance. There are dolerite dyke exposures around all these sites and a perennial source of water. Thus, the site setting agrees well with the settlement pattern of shifting cultivators.

The above analysis of the setting of each site indicates a clear choice of the Neolithic dwellers of the area. The availability of the alluvial deposits with gentle slopes, together with dolerite dyke exposures and a perennial source of water determined the location of these sites. Due to population pressure in recent times Garo settlements have come up in the higher ridges also but the rocky hill slopes are still not preferred for cultivation or habitation.

In the sites situated in the uplands like Didami, Missimagiri and Bibragiri and at Mokbol Bichik situated at a slightly lower level there are no ground and polished tools. On this basis it is inferred that the authors of this assemblage were non-agriculturist. These sites are very close to the steep slopes and the highest contours of the Tura range of mountains. Tropical evergreen forest with luxuriant vegetation and rich species diversity covers these slopes and tropical moist deciduous forest covers the slightly lower ridges.

The resources in the uplands are much more stable. Faunal and floral resources necessary for food and shelter are available almost in all seasons. Tropical regions experience a dry season usually in the winter. Most of the streams and rivulets, which are sources of drinking water dry up. In the uplands these sources usually retain water even in the dry season. It is also possible that human beings occupied these regions when the gentler slopes downstream was relatively less in height. As a result these areas will be prone to floods. This might have discouraged settlers from these gentler slopes when the landscape was evolving. Gradually with further deposition these slopes gained in height and also in fertility, which made it convenient for human habitation in the later periods.

In the tropics due to extremely fine-grained distribution of resources exploitation of a relatively large home range is necessary (Hutterer 1976: 225). Fine grained resources here mean small patches of resources with wide gaps in between and with strong seasonal variation. In the Ganol-Rongram valley the settlers of Bibragiri, Missimagiri and Mokbol Bichik had access to three different topographical situations. A considerable stretch of upland areas in the form of the Tura and Arbella mountains, the valley between the two mountains and the comparatively flat flood plain of the Ganol river further downstream. Ample resources were thus available to the inhabitants of the area in all the seasons as topographical variation in the area allowed growth of resources in particular patches during particular seasons. A variety of resources can be exploited from a single location. Thus, minimum residential mobility was necessary. The homogeneity of the contents in the lithic assemblage of the area indicates increased sedentism (Binford 1982: 20). As dwelling places the flake-blade tool makers had chosen the upland areas may be to escape from ravaging floods or for other safety reasons while exploiting the resources available either in the hills or in the valley or in the flood plain zone during different seasons. The economic potential of different locations becomes increasingly stabilized. Particular areas are seasonally exploited. Correspondingly, the use made of certain places becomes increasingly repetitive. In the same way the lithic tools needed for extraction of resources also attain homogeneity. Thus, the site setting agrees well with the requirements of a sedentary hunter-gatherer community. The character of the artifact assemblage analysed below will further provide us with more convincing proof.

Artifacts

Anything that has any attributes as a consequence of human activity can be called an artifact. Stone tools, bronze daggers, clay pots, butchered animal bones, carbonized seeds, huts, and all other manifestations of human behaviour that are found in archaeological sites are artifacts (Dunnel and Dancey 1983: 277; Fagan 1987: 101). The archaeological record consists of distribution of artifacts over the land surface. Lithic tools and pottery are the most common artifacts found in the archaeological record. In the Ganol-Rongram valley the archaeological record consists of only lithic tools and pottery. All the lithic tools are made of dolerite, which was the only suitable raw material available. Dolerite dyke exposures are prolific in the area and also dolerite river pebbles were used for making tools.

Tools play a strong part in the way people adapt to their surroundings, external, environmental factors and internal social needs. The technology utilized by a group is the outcome of decisions concerning firstly the initial design of the tools and secondly the technology must fit in and adapt to the overall goals set by people and the constraints under which they inevitably operate (Torrence 1989: 1-6).

The local conditions of the Ganol-Rongram valley favoured no choice of raw material. Dolerite was available in great quantity and also in close proximity. The development of tool technology in the area was inevitably influenced by these factors. The dyke material was available in square or rectangular blocks in varying thickness and the river pebbles were round or oval shaped in different sizes. A study on the typology of the tools of the Ganol-Rongram valley has indicated the presence of three varieties of assemblages. They are:

(i) The celt assemblage

(ii) The core tool assemblage and

(iii) The flake-blade assemblage. Assemblage here is used to define typologically similar tools. For this study a total number of 789 artifacts were examined. Thirty-three typological varieties were identified.

Description of each type is presented below. The principal typology followed here is that of Francois Bordes for the core and flake-blade tool assemblages. Unlike the Palaeolithic for which well established typological list are available from each continent (Tixier 1963; Bordes 1961; de Sonneville-Bordes and Perrot 1954-56; Clarke 1978; Debenath and Dibble 1994; Leakey 1935) there is no well established type list for the Neolithic or more precisely for the terminal Pleistocene-Early Holocene cultures of South Asia. For the Neolithic classifications made by Worman (1949), Allchin (1959), Dani (1960), Sharma

(1966a), Rosen (1997) has been used. For the artifacts with Southeast Asian affinities classification made by Bellwood (1978), Higham (1989), Tan Ha Van (1994) have been used.

The description of individual specimens begins with an initial reading of the flake scars. The presence of thick patina on some of the artifacts has blurred the flake scars and retouching and edge damage patterns. Artifacts recovered from Rongram IB, Gawak Abri, Chitra Abri and Mokbol Bichik I have very thick patinas. This maybe because in these sites the vegetation cover is absent. Gawak Abri at present is covered with vegetation but it has been regularly cleared for cultivation and Mokbol Bichik I is a surface site. At Rongram IB and Gawak Abri the artifacts are in contact with water as rainwater leaches down easily encouraging the growth of patina. On the basis of the artifacts from the other sites with minimum patination and the cores and blanks recovered an attempt will be made to reconstruct the reduction sequence of each assemblage for an understanding of the techniques of tool manufacturing in the area. This might give a clear idea of the goals set by the people and the conditions to which they adopted.

(i) The celt assemblage

This assemblage is the first reported lithic assemblage from Northeast India and from Garo hills in particular. It was first reported from Garo Hills in 1931 by G.D. Walker and systematic studies has been undertaken from then by various workers (Mills 1937; Dani 1955, 1960; Goswami and Bhagabati 1957; Sharma 1966b, 1968, 1970,1971,1977; Rao 1980; Mahanta 1995). During the latter half of the last century workers have reported the presence of tools belonging to this assemblage upon any stretch of bare ground on the hill slopes, where they are usually exposed when the areas are cleared for shifting cultivation. This implies that these are either surface or sub surface sites.

The typological classification of this assemblage proposed by previous writers is as follows:

40

(1) the flat celts or hoe blades and

(2) the tanged or shouldered celts. Brief reference to chipped celts is occasionally made but they have not been studied as an individual unit.

In the present study this assemblage is typologically divided into three sub assemblages. They are:

(i) Fully ground and polished celts (Plate 10)

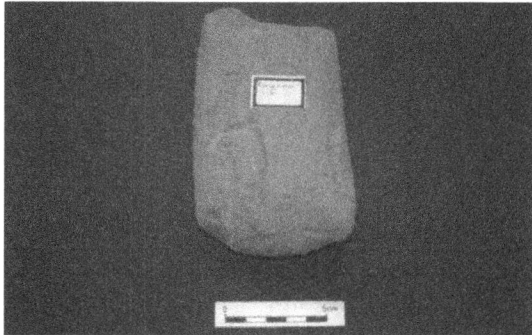

Plate 10: Ground and Polished Celt from Rongram IB

(ii) Partially ground celts (Plate 11)

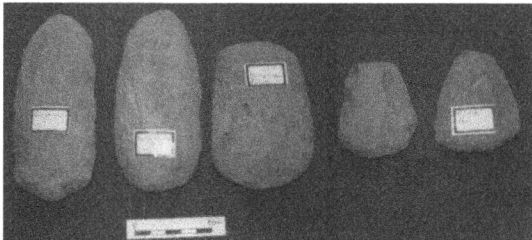

Plate 11: Partially Ground Celts from Rongram IB

(iii) Chipped celts (Plate 12)

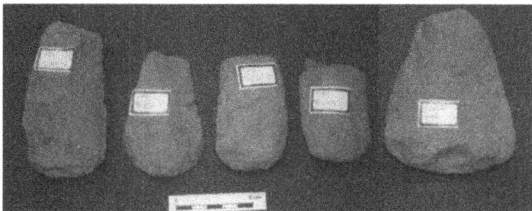

Plate 12: Chipped Celts

In the exploration undertaken under the present study the fully ground and polished celts were found at RongramIB and at Chitra Abri. At Rongaram IB these were found in a buried context and at Chitra Abri they were found exposed on the bed rock with a lot of probably utilised flakes and flake blanks.

This indicated that the dolerite dyke material was utilised for making these tools at Chitra Abri. Partially ground celts were found half buried in the yellowish brown alluvium at RongramIB site and at Ida Bichik. Chipped celts were also found in a half buried context at Ida Bichik. From Gawak Abri and RongramIB chipped celts were recovered from a fully buried context. All the artifacts of this assemblage are heavily patinated. The thick patina on the tools makes it difficult to identify any part of the cortex for which it is difficult to ascertain the morphology of the raw material. Another aspect to be noted is that typologically similar artifacts are found in different context. In all the sites with these celts flakes have also been found some of which were probably utilised. They will be discussed separately under the heading 'flake-blade assemblage'.

There are three varieties of fully ground and polished celts. They are:

(1) the flat celts or hoe blades

(2) the shouldered celts and

(3) the short axes.

The flat celts are called hoes on the basis that the modern iron-hoe blade of the Garos is an exact copy of the stone celt. Also the flat and thin size of the tools with there normally unifacially ground cutting edge make them suitable as agricultural or horticultural tool and not much suitable for felling trees. The curvilinear shouldered celts must have been made for the convenience of hafting. The thick patina has completely hidden the edge damage patterns, which might have given us a clear idea of their functions. Some of the chipped celts show a working edge bisecting the tool in cross section and also they are much thicker in size. They can be called axes. But the narrow rectangular chipped celt must have been used as adzes. Description of each type is given below:

1. Fully ground and polished celt (Fig. 6): They are elongated oval or rectangular in shape with a straight or curved working edge. The sides, butt and cutting edge of the rectangular celts are somewhat conversely

curved in outline. The butt end is square or rectangular. The transverse section is usually biconvex lens shaped, oval or plano-convex and the profile line is almost straight or slightly wavy. This type is found on the surface, sub-surface and also buried context. They are all thickly patinated. They are found at Rongram IB, Ida Bichik, Chitra Abri and Selbalgiri.

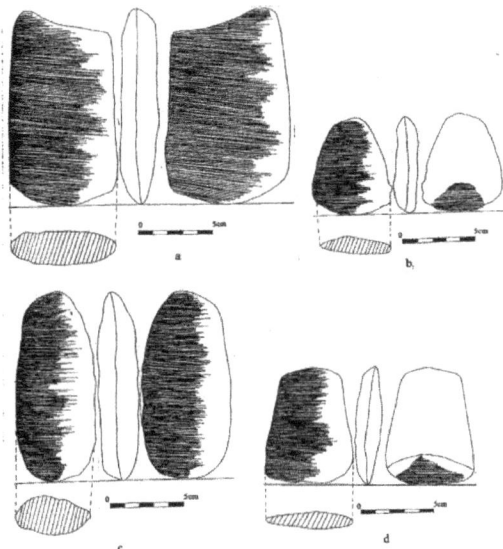

Figure 6: Fully Ground and Polished Celts

2. Fully ground and polished shouldered celts (Fig. 7): These are roughly triangular celts with curvilinear shoulders and a rounded working edge. The butt end is prolonged into a tenon. The transverse section is roughly rectangular or lenticular and the profile line is wavy. These tools are also found on surface, sub-surface or buried context in thickly patinated condition.

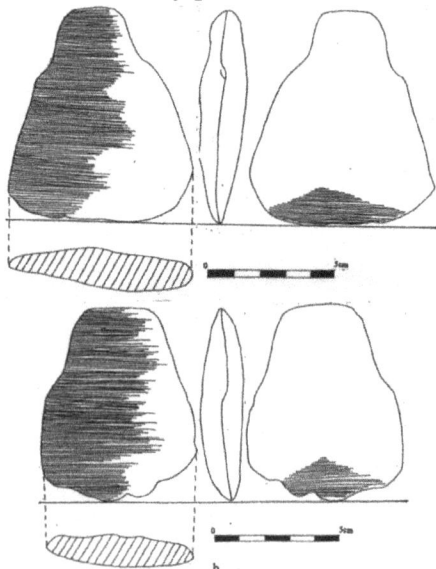

Figure 7: Ground and Polished Shouldered Celts

3. Fully ground and polished short axe (Fig. 8): These are half-cut round, oval or triangular in shape with a convex circular cutting edge. The working edge is not limited to the distal end but some are extended to the sides. As it is made on a truncated river pebble the butt end is formed by the truncated section. The transverse section is ovoid or biconvex and the profile line is wavy or slightly wavy. They have been found in buried context at Rongram IB and Gawak Abri. A thick patina is visible. Some specimens have a completely flat ventral surface.

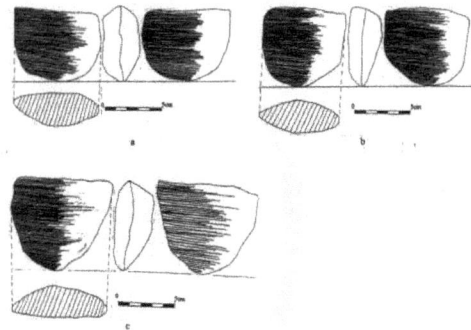

Figure 8: Fully Ground and Polished Short Axes

4. Partially ground celt (Fig. 9): This type of celts are usually rectangular, triangular or elongated oval shaped. The working end is curved. The butt end is square or pointed. The transverse sections are biconvex, biconvex lens shaped, oval or lenticular. Profile lines are slightly wavy, wavy or zig zag. Only some part of the tool is ground while flakes have been removed mainly from the edges from both the dorsal and ventral surface. They are found in sub-surface and in buried context at RongramIB and Gawak Abri. All the specimens are thickly patinated.

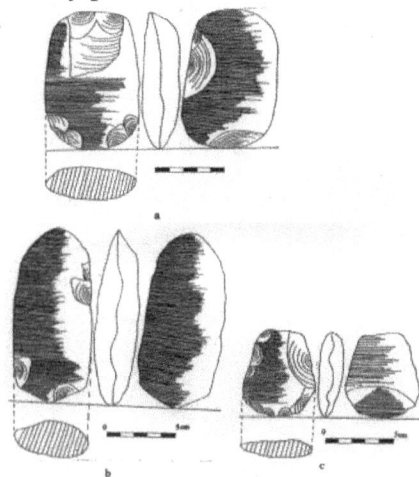

Figure 9: Partially Ground Celts

5. Chipped celt (Fig. 10): These celts are roughly triangular or rectangular in shape. The working end is rounded while the butt end is square. The transverse section is biconvex, concavo convex or plano-convex. The profile line is wavy. The tools are bifacially flaked. Medium and small size shallow flake scars are present on both the dorsal and ventral surface. These are found in sub-surface and buried context at Rongram IB, Gawak Abri and at Ida Bichik. Patination is comparatively less. The working edge bisects the tool in cross section for which it can be called an axe.

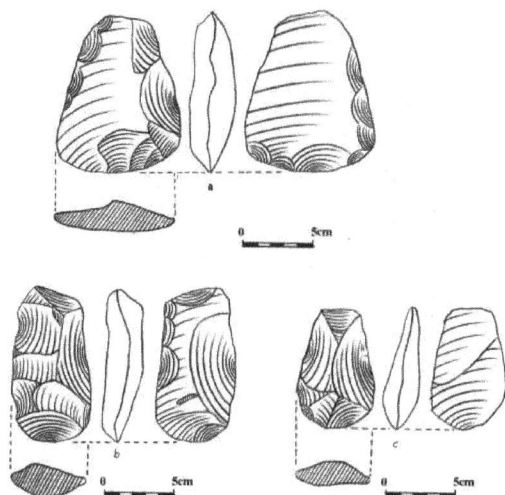

Figure 10: Chipped Celts

Technique

These celts were manufactured on either flakes or flat pebbles. The tools were usually modified such that original blank type is impossible to ascertain. But the different types of celts like the chipped celt, the partially ground celt and the fully ground celt very well indicates different stages of manufacture. On this basis the reduction sequence can be ascertained. Dolerite dyke fragments or pebbles of suitable size were selected and roughly flaked. Flakes are mainly removed from the edges to achieve the desired shape. Round river pebbles found most often with these celts were probably used as hammers. Edges were ground or rough parts were smoothened in the next stage. Many tools have been left at this stage maybe because it was the desired type. Flat celts with sharp working edges were produced when the tool was fully ground and polished. Grinding was usually done on stationery blocks preferably near the river. Sand with water was probably used as an abrasive for grinding and polishing. Two adjacent short corners were ground at times to produce a pair of curvilinear shoulders for the convenience of hafting. Polishing increased with use and resharpening. These flat celts were discarded very often when the edges wear out and the celt is reduced in size. These celts might have been hafted into wooden or bamboo handles for use but no handles have been recovered.

Ground and polished tools are the characteristic tool types of the Neolithic period but edge ground, partially ground and chipped celts have been reported from a slightly earlier context in Southeast Asia. During the Pleistocene-Holocene transition period (12,000-10,000 B.P.) in parts of Southeast Asia certain wild food exploiting cultures developed of which the best known is the Hoabinhian. From the Spirit Cave in northern Thailand and from certain sites in Vietnam the most convincing evidence of a slightly earlier origin of the edge ground and chipped celts has come.

(ii) The core tool assemblage

This includes two sub assemblages. They are:

(i) Pebble tools and

(ii) the Bifaces.

Pebble tool assemblage (Plate13)

This assemblage was first reported from Rongdu located in the northeastern part of Garo hills (*IAR* 1969-70: 3). Within the study area the most convincing evidence has been reported from the Rongram IB site (Sharma 1990: 136-139). At Bibragiri pebble short axes are present. It is noteworthy that in the sites, which are on the banks of the two main rivers pebble tools are found. Bibragiri is on the eastern bank of the Ganol while the Rongram IB site is also on the eastern bank of the Rongram. Availability of river pebbles at close proximity must have encouraged their use as raw material in these particular sites. Short axe is the most common type of pebble tool found in the area. Utilised flakes and chopping tools are the next most common type. At Rongram IB this assemblage occurs within the brown alluvium (7.5yr; 5/8 Munsell colour chart). At Bibragiri short axes only have been found in a half-buried condition in the brown sandy silt along with the flake-blade tools. These axes also occur at Gawak Abri in a fully buried context.

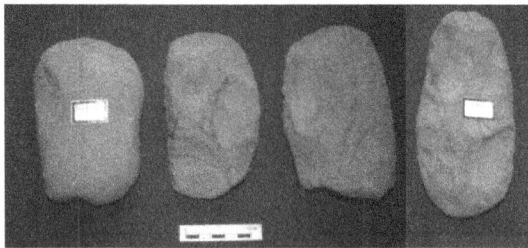

Plate 13: Pebble Tools from Rongram IB

6. Short Axe (Fig. 11, Plate 14): These are half-cut round or oval shaped tools which are made on truncated pebbles. They are characterized by transverse truncation. The transverse section is oval, convex, biconvex or roughly rectangular. The profile line is wavy or slightly wavy. Majority of the flakes has been initiated from the lateral sides. The flakes are shallow and regular. The working edge is rounded and not limited to the distal end but some are extended to the sides. Short axes have been found at Rongram IB, Gawak Abri and Bibragiri.

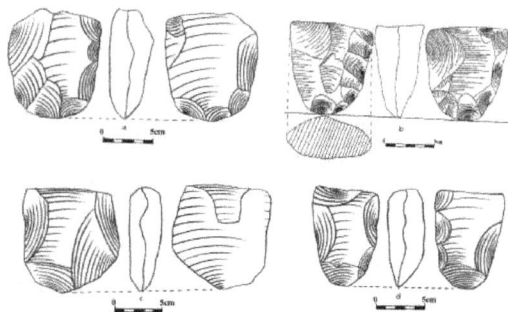

Figure 11: Short Axes

7. Scraper (Fig. 12): These are oval in shape. On the dorsal face a few flakes are removed particularly from the edges and the central part retains the cortex or the original pebble surface. On the ventral surface few flakes are removed only from the right border while the remaining part remains unflaked.

It is thickly patinated. The profile line is wavy and the transverse section is oval lens shaped. The working edge is limited to one of the lateral sides. This edge is prepared by removing flakes from both the dorsal and ventral faces. This scraper type has been found only at the Rongram IB site. The size is uniform.

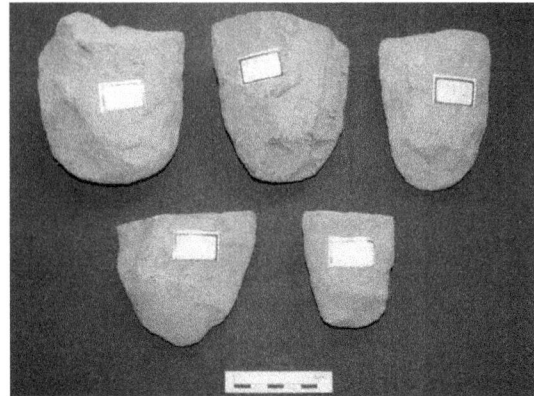

Plate 14: Short Axes from Rongram IB

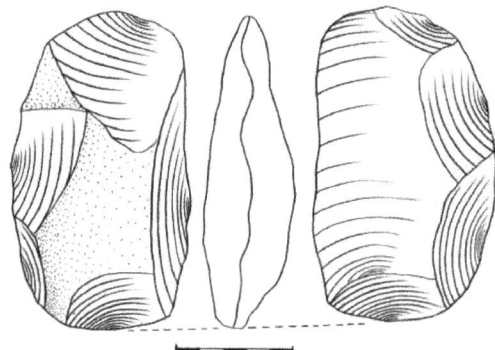

Figure 12: Scraper

8. Partially ground axe (Fig. 13, Plate 15): These are elongated oval shaped pebbles bifacially flaked. On both the dorsal and ventral faces large, medium and small shallow flake scars are removed. The flakes have been removed mainly by striking on the edges. It is partially ground on both the faces. The cross section is convex and the profile line is slightly wavy. A thick patina is present. Both the working end and the butt end are rounded. The butt end is thick while the working end is much thinner. This artifact type has been collected from the Rongram IB site.

44

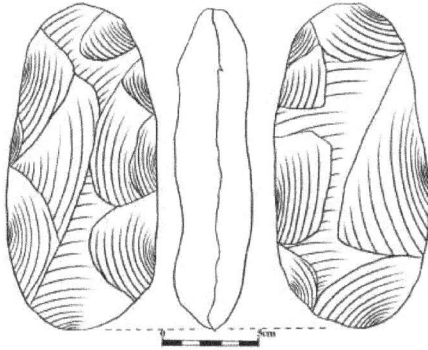

Figure 13: Partially Ground Axe

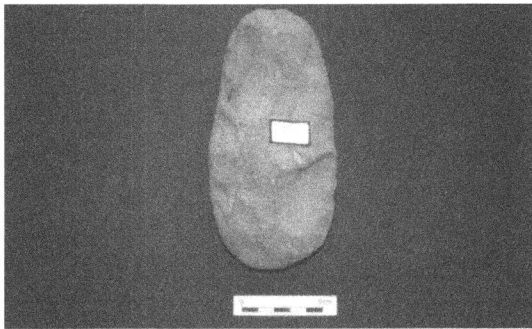

Plate 15: Partially Ground Axe from Rongram IB

9. Pebble chopper (Fig. 14): This tool has been made on a rectangular flattish pebble. On both the dorsal and ventral faces a few flakes have been removed on the working end. The flake scars are deep. The rest of the tool remains unflaked. The profile line is almost straight and the transverse section is oval in shape. Both the working end and the butt end are rounded. Artifacts of this type have been collected from the Rongram IB site.

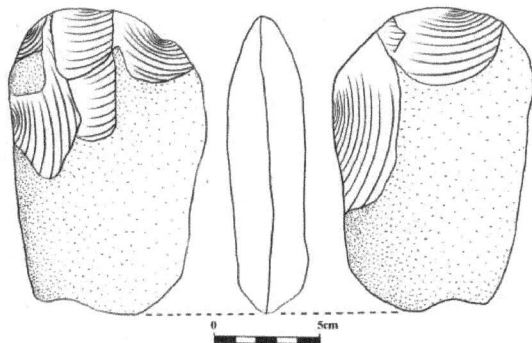

Figure 14: Pebble Chopper

The above description reveals certain characteristic features of this assemblage. The short axes are made on truncated river pebbles, which are bifacially flaked. No prepared striking platform is visible. Large, medium and small size shallow flakes have been removed by striking in the edges for the preparation of a curvilinear working edge. Maximum flaking is visible on the edges while in the center shallow flakes are removed. For the preparation of scrapers and choppers suitable size pebbles are selected and a few flakes removed for preparing the working edge. Major part of the pebble remains untouched or unflaked. On the basis of the size and shape of the flake scars it can be stated that these flakes were removed by direct percussion employing hard hammer.

Bifaces (Plates 16, 17, & 18)

Tools belonging to this assemblage have been prepared on blocks or slabs of dolerite extracted from dykes. They are all bifaces of different shapes. The term biface here is used to define a core blank that has been reduced on both faces from two parallels but opposing axis through percussion and is shaped into a specific form (Kelly 1988:718).

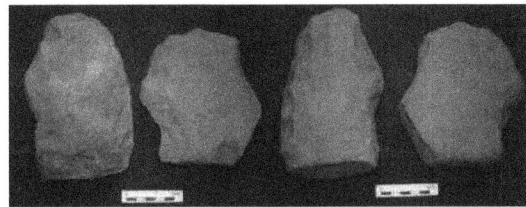

Plate 16: Biface

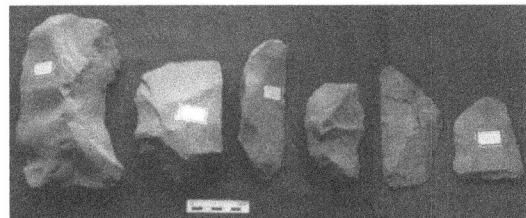

Plate 17: Bifaces made on slabs and Citrus Flake shape Artifacts from Mokbol Bichik I

Plate 18: Bifaces from Didami

(10) Triangular biface (Fig. 15): These have lateral edges that are straight or slightly convex, and generally a straight base. The

base often retains a certain amount of cortex or is naturally blunt. Flakes are removed only from the edges on both the dorsal and ventral faces and the rest of the surface is left untouched. The dorsal surface is convex while the ventral surface is flat. The lateral sides gradually tapers towards the distal end forming a slightly round pointed working end. The profile line is always wavy and the transverse section are biconvex or broadly oval. It is thickly patinated.

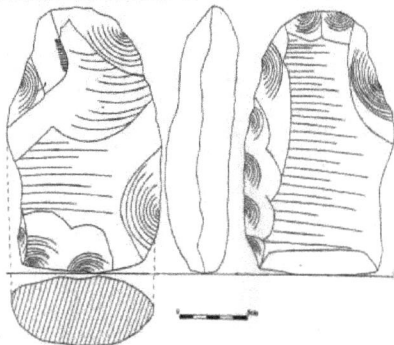

Figure 15: Triangular Biface

These specimens have been recovered from the Rongram IB site only.

(11) Square uniface (Fig. 16): This is made on a roughly square flat slab1.7 cm thick. On the dorsal surface flakes have been removed along the lateral margins. The rest of the area has been left unflaked. Both the dorsal and ventral surfaces are flat. The proximal end is roughly straight while the distal end is convex and rounded. Slight concavity is present on the lateral margins. The tool is thickly patinated because of which it is difficult to ascertain whether the unflaked surface is the cortex. The profile line has a curve and the transverse section is rectangular with a tapering edge.

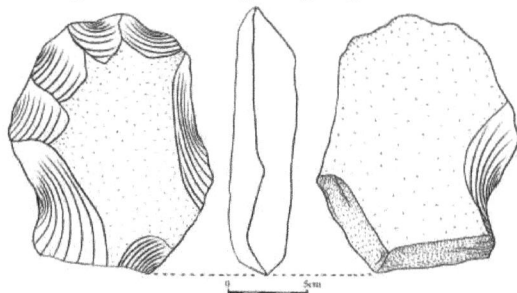

Figure 16: Square Uniface

This type of artifact type has been found from the Rongram IB site.

(12) Square Biface (Fig. 17): This is also made on a square slab 4 cm in thickness.

Flakes have been removed from the proximal end of both the dorsal and ventral surfaces, which is pointed. The distal end is roughly straight. It is formed as a result of the intersection of two flake scars from the dorsal and ventral surface forming a wide cutting edge. One of the lateral margins is completely straight and backed while the opposite margin is convex and comparatively sharp. The profile line is straight while the transverse section is elongated wedge shaped. Patination is thick. Three of these pieces were collected from Rongram IB site.

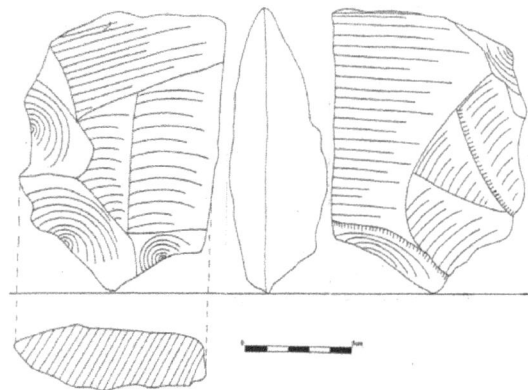

Figure 17: Square Biface

(13) Stemmed Scrapper (Fig. 18): This artifact has also been made on a slab, which is 2.2 cm thick. The ventral surface is flat and retouching is visible on the proximal end, which is straight. The rest of the ventral surface is unflaked. Flakes have been removed from the lateral margins of the dorsal surface. The right lateral margin is straight and backed. The working edge extends from the distal end to the upper half of the left lateral margin, which is slightly concave. The lower half of the left lateral margin slopes down and forms a pointed proximal end. This is the stem. The stem is defined as a more or less isolated protrusion, usually on the proximal part of the flake, formed by direct percussion from either the interior or exterior surface. The profile line is wavy and it has a wedge shaped transverse section. Patination is minimum or absent. This artifact type made on slabs have been found from Mokbol Bichik and Bibragiri.

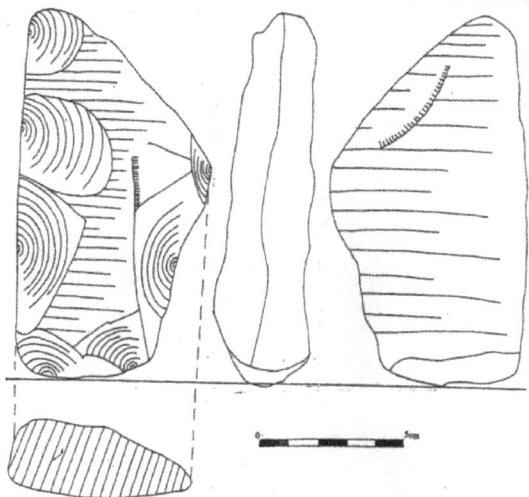

Figure 18: Stemmed Scrapper

(14) Concave scrapper (Figs. 19 a & b, Plate 19):

(a) This specimen is made on a slab and has a convex dorsal surface and relatively flat ventral surface. One of the lateral edge is concave. It is a rectangular shape block with a truncated proximal end. Large size flakes have been removed from the dorsal surface mainly along the edges. The concave edge is made by removing a large deep flake on the dorsal surface. On the ventral surface a few flakes have been removed only from the distal end. The profile line is wavy and the transverse section is bi-convex. No patina.

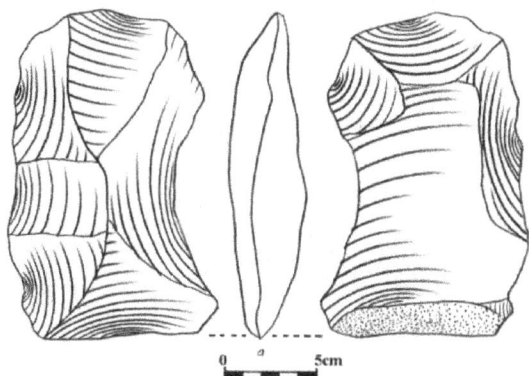

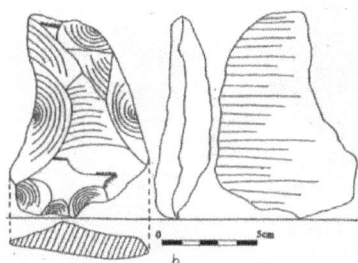

Figure 19: Concave Scraper

Plate 19: Probably utilised Flakes with a Concave edge from Bibragiri

(b) This artifact made on a slab has a convex dorsal surface and a flat ventral surface. One of the lateral edges is concave and the opposite edge is convex. It is roughly crescent shaped. Flakes have been removed only from the dorsal surface while the ventral surface is unflaked. The distal end is pointed beak like while the proximal end is comparatively straight. The profile line is wavy and the transverse section is biconvex. This type of artifacts frequently occurs at Rongram IB, Mokbol Bichik, Bibragiri, Missimagiri and Didami.

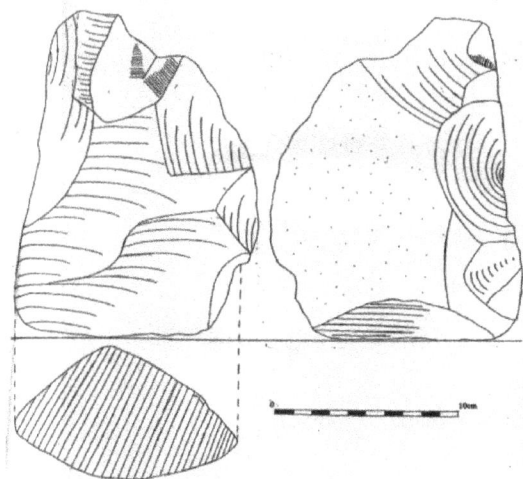

Figure 20: Convex Scraper

(15) Convex Scraper (Fig. 20): This is bifacially flaked with one straight lateral margin, a slightly convex tip, and a tranchet that originates from the distal end. The opposite edge is most often convex and thick, attaining its maximum thickness at about the middle or proximal two-thirds of the piece. In plan form they are generally D-shaped. Tools resembling this description are found at Mokbol Bichik I and II, and

Bibragiri and Didami. The thickness of the straight edge is deliberately reduced by removing a few flakes. The transverse section is wedge shaped and the profile line is slightly wavy. Patination is minimum.

(16) Hachoirs (Fig. 21): Bordes defined them as thick flakes, with a straight or slightly convex bifacially retouched cutting edge at their distal end. Usually the bifacial edge is more or less irregular. This term covers various objects, from large bifacial scrapers to chopping tools. This definition also encompasses truncated-faceted pieces. The specimen described here is a truncated piece with a convex bifacially retouched cutting edge. Flakes have been removed from the proximal and distal end of the dorsal surface but some part of the cortex is visible. The distal and lateral edges on both the dorsal and ventral surfaces have been retouched for preparation of the working edge. The ventral surface is completely flaked. In the absence of the positive bulb on the ventral surface it is difficult to identify it as a flake. It can be called a modified block. On the basis of the negative bulb on the ventral surface it can also be called a modified core. The transverse section is biconvex and the profile line is wavy. Patination is minimum. They occur commonly at Didami.

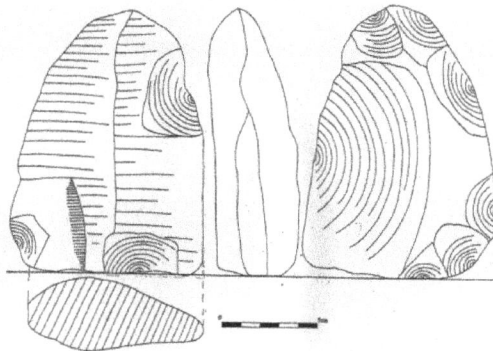
Figure 21: Hachoirs

(17) Abrupt scraper/knife (Fig. 22): According to Bordes these are pieces with scraper retouch that is abrupt or semi-abrupt. The difference between an abrupt scraper and a backed knife with abrupt retouch is that an abrupt knife must have a sharp and unretouched cutting edge opposite the abrupt edge. If the edge opposite the abrupt edge is retouched or not suitable for cutting then the piece should be classified as a scraper. In this piece the edge opposite to the abrupt edge is unretouched but sharp. Thus, it can be called a backed knife with abrupt retouch. It has a truncated proximal end and a convex working edge. It is bifacially flaked. The transverse section is roughly rectangular with a tapering edge and the profile line is wavy. No patina is noticed. This type of artifacts has been collected from Mokbol Bichik.

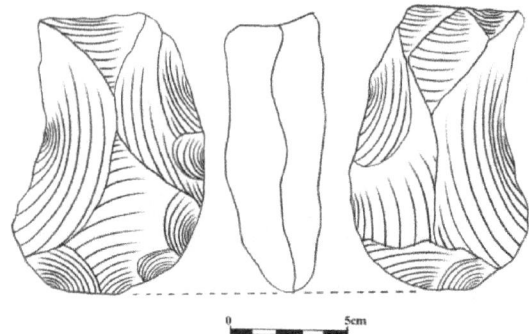
Figure 22: Abrupt Scraper/Knife

(18) Bevelled Biface (Fig. 23): For those cleaver like objects whose distal cutting edge is produced by multiple flake scars whether bifacial or unifacial and from whatever directions the term bevelled biface is applied. The specimen described here, collected from Didami, is a totally bifacially worked implement, which has a thin, transverse cutting edge at the distal end, analogus to a cleaver edge. The cutting edge made by intentional flaking is almost straight. The butt end is square and thick. The profile line is wavy and the transverse section is roughly rectangular. Patination is minimum.

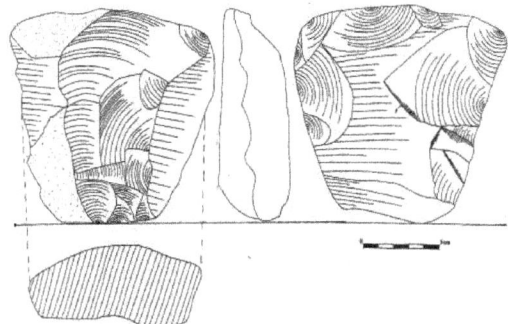
Figure 23: Bevelled Biface

From the above description certain characteristic feature of these bifaces can be noted. Majority of them can be classified under well-defined typological shapes. A truncated proximal end is a common feature, which is often confused as a part of the striking platform. But in the absence of a positive bulb of percussion there is little doubt that these are truncated blocks. Usually only 30%-50% of the total area of the selected block is flaked for the preparation of the artifact. Flaking is done mainly on the edges on both the dorsal and ventral sides. The rest of the area is left untouched. In fact these tools can be called edge retouched bifacial tools. Only a few are completely flaked on both the faces. The average thickness of the dolerite dyke blocks chosen for making tools varies from 5 cm to 20 cm. The length varies from 10 cm to 30 cm. They disintegrate into roughly rectangular or square blocks by natural process of weathering. For the preparation of an artifact uniform size blocks are easily available. Otherwise larger blocks are divided into two or more halves as required. This results in the platform like surface on the proximal end. Actually such a surface is present all around the tool. But as a result of flaking the surface disappears from at least two edges while as flaking is rarely done on the butt end it retains the original surface.

(iii) The flake-blade tool assemblage.

Flakes can be defined as any objects detached from larger stone masses essentially possessing a positive bulb and a platform indicating human intent (Cotterell and Kamminga 1987: 675-708). Any flake with sharp parallel edges and the length of which is twice its breadth can be called a blade. The blade-like flakes to be described below possess sharp parallel edges but the length is not always twice its breadth. Thus, they are called blade like flakes. Artifacts within this assemblage can be classified under the well defined typological categories but in the absence of retouch in a majority of them classification is not free from doubts. It is safer to refer them as probably utilised flakes. In the texts these are referred by figure numbers only.

For matter of convenience the whole assemblage will be divided into two parts. In the first part the flakes which have been found in association with the Neolithic tools will be described and in the second part the typical flake-blade assemblage of the area will be described. The second group has been called typical on the basis that at certain sites of the study area in a particular stratigraphic context, artifacts belonging to this assemblage specifically occur with the bifaces. They outnumber the bifaces thus forming a dominant group.

Flakes found with the Neolithic tools are (Plate 20)

Plate 20: Probably Utilised flakes found within the Neolithic Context from Gawak Abri

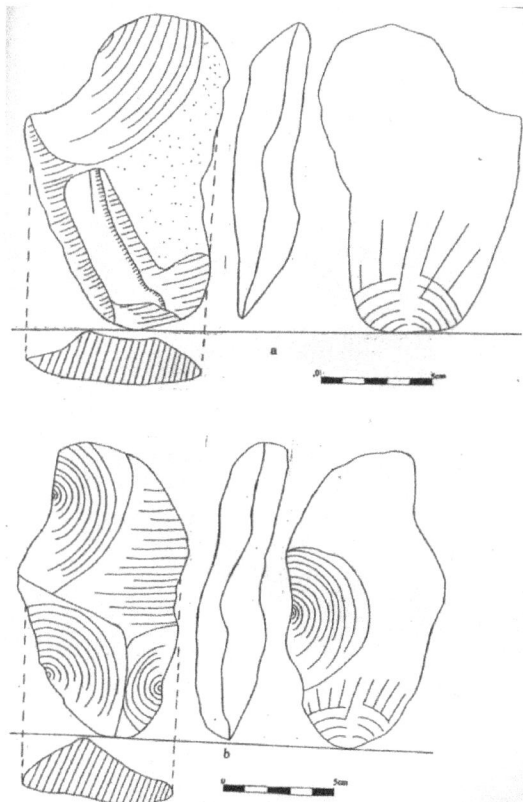

Figure 24: Probably Utilised Flakes

19. Figs. 24 a and b: Both the flakes are roughly oval in shape. The dorsal surface is irregularly flaked and on the ventral surface the positive bulb of percussion is present. In specimen (b) part of the bulb is removed by flaking. The end opposite the bulb is the

working or distal end. A big flake has been removed abruptly on the right corner of the distal end resulting in the formation of a concave edge. These flakes found at Rongram IB site look like concave scrapers, which may have been hafted. Two deep flakes are usually removed along the edges in the mid-region of the flakes. This may have been done for the convenience of hafting.

20. Figs. 25 a, b, c and d: These are triangular shaped flakes less than 2 cm in breadth. The length of the flakes ranges between 2 cm to 3 cm. Flake scars are present on the dorsal surface while the positive bulb of percussion on the ventral surface is subdued or absent. On the basis of the position of the bulb it is presumed that the pointed tip was the working end. Fifteen such pieces were collected from Gawak Abri. From ethnographic data it is known that metal tips of similar shape, was used as arrowheads by the locals in the recent past. These pieces were thickly patinated.

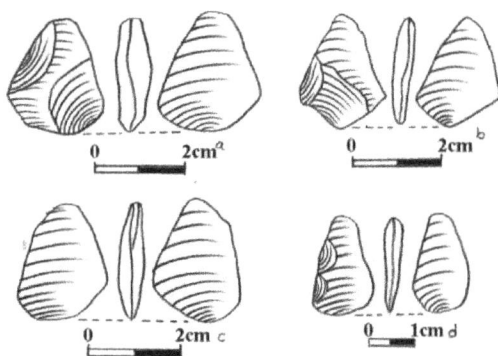

Figure 25: Probably Utilised Flakes

21. Fig. 26: This flake is shaped like the English alphabet 'D' with a pedestaled lower part. The maximum breadth is 2.8 cm and the maximum length is 3.9 cm. On the curved edge, which is sharp, just below the mid-point there is a notch. The positive bulb of percussion on the ventral side is very prominent. In fact the size of the bulb suggests that it was a much bigger flake, which must have reduced in size with incessant use. As one of its lateral edges is sharp it can be called a side scraper and the presence of the knot suggest hafting. From Gawak Abri five such thickly patinated pieces were found.

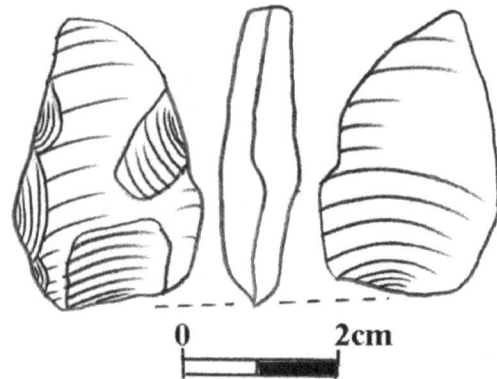

Figure 26: Probably Utilised Flakes

22. Fig. 27: This flake is crescent shape with a wide proximal end and a narrow distal end. The maximum breadth is 2 cm and the length is 3.5 cm. Flakes have been removed from the dorsal surface and the right lateral edge is concave. The bulb of percussion on the ventral side has been partially removed by flaking. It can be called a small size concave scraper. In the lithic assemblage of Gawak Abri this type frequently occurs.

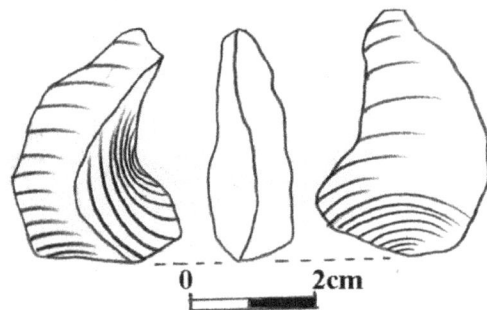

Figure 27: Probably Utilised Flakes

23. Fig. 28: It is a side struck flake, 1.7 cm in length and 2.8 cm in breadth. It is roughly triangular in shape. One of the longer sides of the triangle, opposite the positive bulb is straight and sharp. In spite of the patina abrasion on this side can be noticed. Probably this was a scraping edge and this is one piece of a composite tool.

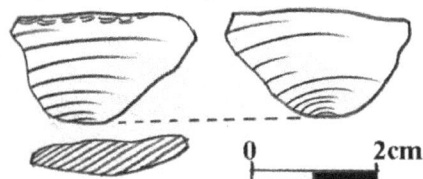

Figure 28: Probably Utilised Flakes

24. Figs. 29 a and b: These are blade like flakes. The length of specimen (a) is 3.7 cm and (b) is 2.6 cm. The breadth is 1.7 cm and

1.1 cm respectively. Twelve such pieces were found at Gawak Abri.

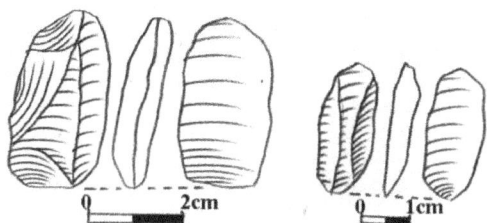

Figure 29: Probably Utilised Flakes

The flakes from Gawak Abri has been found in association with potsherds, chipped celts, short axes and ground and polished celts. They can be called probably utilised flakes. The most distinctive character of these flakes is their small size. But in some of the specimens it was noticed that in comparison to the flake the positive bulb was much larger in size and it was almost in the center of the ventral surface. This indicates that the flakes were much bigger and have reduced in size due to excessive use. An analysis of the size of the flakes found in the site revealed uniformity in size. Assuming that the archaeological record consists of the discarded flakes, it can be inferred that after the flakes were reduced to a particular size they were discarded. Besides these discarded flakes a considerable number of flake blanks of similar size also form part of the assemblage. In the assemblage under study from Gawak Abri there are no cores. But in an excavation conducted by the Dept. of Anthropology, Gauhati University in the year 1976 on the same site a few cores were found. These were roughly cylindrical cores with a prepared platform at either ends. The body of the core, though prepared, is often left uneven which actually guides the length and breadth of the flakes removed. Often the mid-region of the body of the core bulges out. This might be deliberately retained to restrict the size of the flake. Flakes were removed by striking on the platform vertically. These were usually blade flakes but some amorphous flakes were also removed. The diameters of these cores ranged between 6 cm and 7 cm. Flakes measuring 2 cm to 3 cm in length and less in breadth were removed by striking on the platforms. Uniformity is noticed in the size of the flakes. This indicates that the force applied was controlled. It was a prepared core technique.

Pottery

Two types of handmade dull grey plain pottery was found in the same context. Of this one was coarse and gritty variety (Plate 21) while there was a thin wash on the surface of the other (Plate 22) variety on account of which it looked finer. The potsherds recovered are very small in size which makes reconstruction of the shapes difficult. No clay source could be identified in the study area. Also the use of not so well levigated clay indicates that poor quality clay was used mixed with quartz grits. The pots were fire baked.

Plate 21: Pottery with a thin wash from Gawak Abri

Plate 22: Coarse and Gritty variety pottery from Gawak Abri

Typical flake-blade assemblage (Plates 23 & 24)

Plate 23: Probably utilised flakes from Bibragiri

Plate 24: Blade Flakes and Amorphous Flakes from Didami

25. Fig. 30: This is a side struck flake with a prominent positive bulb of percussion and striking platform. The end opposite to the bulb is the longest and concave. The breadth of the flake is more than the length. A few flakes have been struck off from the dorsal surface while no flaking has been done on the ventral side.

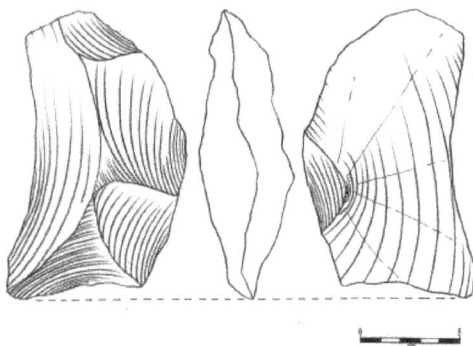

Figure 30: Probably Utilised Flakes

The profile line is slightly wavy and the transverse section is wedge-shaped. Probably the concave end was used for scraping. These types of flakes frequently occur in the tool assemblage of Mokbol Bichik. It has a patina.

26. Fig. 31: These are roughly square size flat flakes with a subdued bulb. The dorsal surface is flaked and the right upper corner is heavily flaked to form a half 'U' shape deep concave cutting edge. The transverse section is lenticular and the profile line is bow shaped. These are found in profuse numbers at Bibragiri. From a grid of 5 m x 5 m twenty such pieces, complete and broken were collected. Probably they were also used as concave scrapers. It is not patinated.

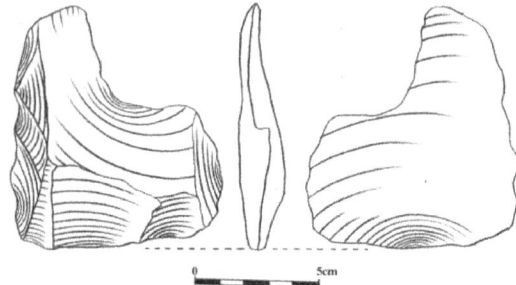

Figure 31: Probably Utilised Flakes

27. Fig. 32: These are rectangular flakes of different sizes with a prominent bulb and striking platform. One of the lateral edges is sharp while the opposite edge is naturally backed. They are unretouched flakes or blades that have a sharp cutting edge on one margin and a natural cortical surface on the opposing edge, which is perpendicular or nearly so, to the interior surface. Elongated blade like flakes have been removed from the dorsal surface while the ventral surface has been left untouched. Both the lateral margins bend towards the left and join together to form a beak like point which also may have been probably used. The profile line is almost straight while the transverse section is wedge shaped or trapezoid. It is patinated. These flakes fit into Bordes definition of naturally backed knives. At the site of Mokbol Bichik maximum number of these flakes occur.

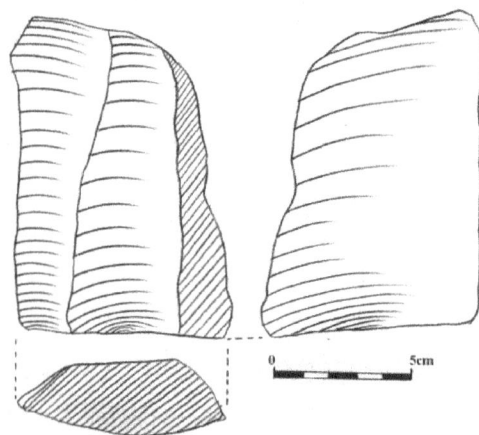

Figure 32: Probably Utilised Flakes

52

28. Fig. 33: This flake is shaped like the English alphabet 'D'. The straight lateral side is blunted. The dorsal surface is flaked while no flakes are removed from the ventral surface. It is a side-struck flake and the blunted straight edge maybe the part of the striking platform. The edge opposite to the blunted edge is convex. No retouching is present on the edges for which this can be called a probably utilised flake. The transverse section is quadrilateral in shape and the profile line is slightly wavy. Seven such specimens were collected from Bibragiri and from Mokbol Bichik three were collected.

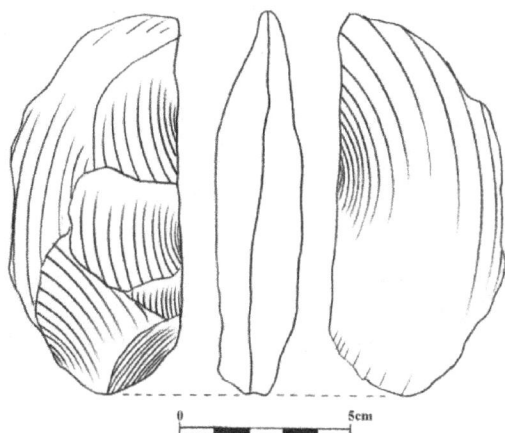

Figure 33: Probably Utilised Flakes

29. Fig. 34: Though this type has been classified under the flake-blade assemblage in the absence of a positive bulb it is doubtful if this can be called a flake. But the absence of the positive bulb can be attributed to the peculiar technique of flake manufacture. These citrus slice shaped flakes are made by splitting river pebbles or similar blocks into thick halves. Thus, one lateral edge is naturally backed. A few flakes have been removed from the dorsal surface of the backed edge may be for the convenience of holding it. It has a wide cutting edge and is bigger than the normal citrus flakes reported from the Middle Palaeolithic context of Europe and Upper Palaeolithic context of India.

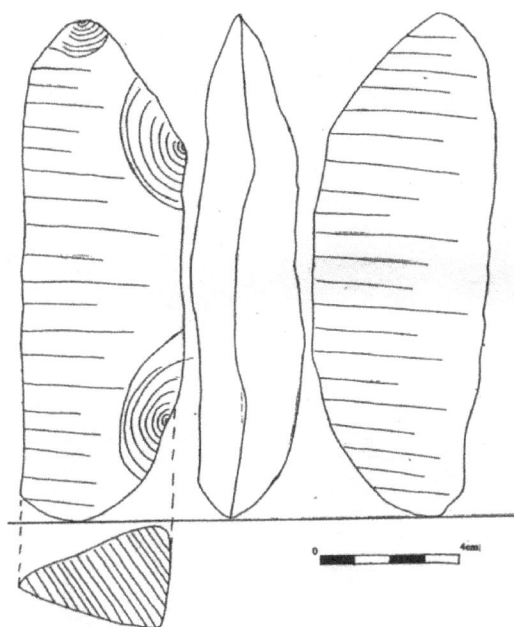

Figure 34: Probably Utilised Flakes

30. Fig. 35: This is a thick flake with a prominent positive bulb and striking platform. No flakes have been removed from the ventral surface. The dorsal surface is completely flaked. The right lateral edge is almost straight and naturally backed while the curved edge opposite to it is sharp. The profile line is almost straight and the transverse section is wedge-shaped. Probably this was used as a scraper. These types were found at Bibragiri and Didami.

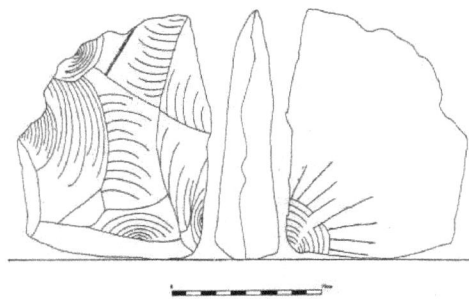

Figure 35: Probably Utilised Flakes

31. Figs. 36 a, b, c, d and e: These are triangular flakes with a central or medial ridge, sometimes possessing a triangle at the base. A few of them are slightly elongated. The end opposite the positive bulb is pointed. Majority of the transverse sections are wedge-shaped and bi-convex. The profile lines are slightly wavy. They are undoubtedly pointed tools. They closely resemble the Levallois points with a mid-rib. It is difficult to assess whether the points are

53

retouched due to the presence of thick patina. They occur profusely at Bibragiri and Didami. Almost seventy percent of the artifacts from Bibragiri are of this type.

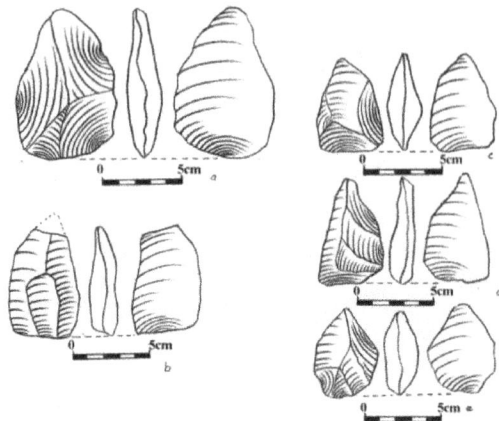

Figure 36: Probably Utilised Flakes

32. Figs. 37 a, b, c, d, e, f and g: These are flakes of uniform size but varied shapes. They are thin relative to their length and width, and have fairly flat exterior surfaces. The presence of the positive bulb and part of the striking platform in some of them clearly indicates that these are products of a prepared core technique. The transverse sections are mostly bi-convex while profile lines are straight and slightly wavy. One part of the lateral edge or distal end is sharp. This may be the working end. At Bibragiri and Didami these flakes are quite common. The degree of patination is less.

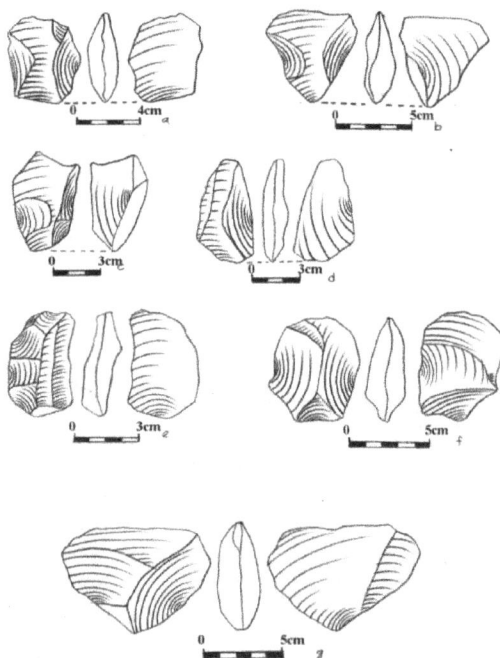

Figure 37: Probably Utilised Flakes

33. Figs. 38 a, b, c, d, e and f: These are blade-like flakes. They cannot be called pure blades because their length is not always twice the breadth. These flakes have sharp parallel edges. On the dorsal surface straight parallel ridges are seen. The positive bulb of percussion is prominent. The transverse sections are bi-convex and lenticular and the profile lines are almost straight or slightly wavy. Almost sixty percent of the assemblage at Missimagiri, Bibragiri and Didami consists of this type of flakes. Study of cores collected from Didami, Gawak Abri and Missimagiri contributed to the understanding of the technique of flake production.

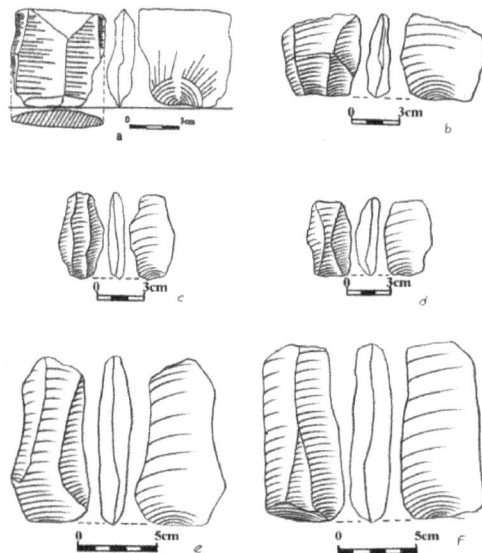

Figure 38: Probably Utilised Flakes

Tabular cores are common (Plate 25): These are made on dolerite boulders. Two platforms are seen at the two poles of a boulder. Usually one platform is prepared while the other is unprepared. It is partially dressed but no attempt is made to prepare a cylindrical nodule. From the negative bulbs it can be estimated that two types of flakes were produced from the same core. From one side blade flakes were removed while from another side flakes of irregular shapes were removed. A few of the negative bulbs were very deep. This must have been possible because of the nature of the raw material. The direction of the force applied was almost vertical. As dolerite is a very hard material it is quite difficult to dress a boulder to complete cylindrical shape necessary for the removal of blades. Thus, from the part of the core, which could be dressed blade-flakes were produced and from the rest of the core flakes of amorphous shapes were produced. The flakes were homogeneous in size. A comparative analysis of the flakes from Gawak Abri, Mokbol Bichik, Bibragiri and Didami shows that the flakes from Mokbol Bichik are slightly bigger in size while the flakes from Bibragiri and Didami are almost similar in size. This indicates planning by the tool makers. The technique was undoubtedly a prepared core technique showing indigenous development of technology in the area.

Plate 25: Tabular Core from Didami

Conclusion

From the above description it is clear that the pattern of the spatially continuous archaeological record of the Ganol-Rongram valley conforms to the distribution of resources in the area. All the sites are within a range of 300 m from the nearest dolerite dyke and near a perennial source of water. But the immediate vicinity of the main river Ganol and its tributary the Rongram was avoided by the Stone Age people of the area. Majority of the sites are found within the deposits created by the first order and second order streams. Only Rongram IB and Bibragiri are two sites which are on deposits created by the Rongram and Ganol respectively. This choice must have been made to avoid the menacing flood waters during the rainy season. The altitude of Bibragiri prevents flooding of the site while at Rongram the river divides into two channels. This reduces the intensity of the flood waters. Also the site setting clearly focuses on the 'home range'.

Around each Neolithic site in the valley a considerable amount of cultivable land is present. The setting of the sites matches closely with the settlement pattern of the present day shifting cultivators of the area. The fertile alluvial deposits with gentle slopes suitable for cultivation were chosen for habitation.

The typological analysis of the artifacts indicates that the Neolithic celts were agricultural tools. Edge damage in a few of them and their small size suggest that they were discarded after heavy use. Sixty percent of the flakes found with the Neolithic tools possess positive bulbs much larger then usually seen on flakes of this size. From this it can be ascertained that the sizes of both the types of artifacts have reduced as a result of incessant use. Thus, the tools were discarded after their utility reduced to the minimum. On the basis of this discard behaviour certain inferences can be made.

(1) Even though raw material was easily available there was some amount of curation. Curation is a strategy of caring for tools and tool kits and has various dimensions. Reshaping and caching or storage are a few of them (Nelson 1991: 62). Dolerite, the raw material used in the study area is a difficult material for making tools. Thus, once a required shape was successfully made it was preserved. When efficiency dropped it was resharpened and used. It was discarded when it could no longer be resharpened.

(2) It might also be so that most of the specialised tools were made of organic material. The lithic tools were only processing tools. Thus, the energy and time invested in the procurement of the lithic artifacts was restricted to the minimum. This encouraged resharpening.

The presence of potsherds with the artifacts at Gawak Abri indicates food processing and storage. But the absence of data on dwelling structures and use of plant and animal foods creates a lacunae in the archaeological record. From the typology of the lithic tools, one can envisage a group of people practising agriculture on the hills, using lithic tools but economising on their production, probably possessing a material culture dominated by artifacts made out of wood, bamboo etc and processing and storing food in earthen pots. Their behaviour on the landscape must have concentrated around these activities resulting in the formation of the archaeological record.

The density and distribution of the flake-blade assemblage clearly reflect pattern of resource utilisation. From Bibragiri, Missimagiri, Mokbol Bichik and Didami the authors of this assemblage had access to three different topographical situations. a) a considerable stretch of upland areas in the form of the Tura and Arbella mountains; b) the valley in between the two mountains; and c) the comparatively flat flood plain of the Ganol river further downstream. Ample resources were thus available to the inhabitants of the area in all the seasons as topographical variation in the area allowed growth of resources in particular patches during particular seasons. Thus, the site setting agrees well with the requirements of a sedentary hunter-gatherer community. The character of the artifact assemblage analysed has provided us with more convincing proof. The homogeneity and density of the artifacts indicate stability of resources and repeated use of the sites. Increased sedentism, spending greater amount of time in one place, leads to expediently planned technology because of the cumulative availability of material (Nelson 1991: 80). Artifacts in this assemblage consist of unretouched medium size flakes and blade flakes. This indicates economic use of the raw material (Hayden 1989: 9) which was not necessary. Thus, the presence of a group of hunter-gatherers who produced flakes and blade flakes by a prepared core technique and also used bifacial and pebble tools in the Ganol-Rongram valley can be postulated.

Within India the typical flake-blade assemblage with the pebble short axes and the bifaces have no parallel. This assemblage and the bifaces and pebble tools belong to the same geological context. Short axe, the most frequently occurring pebble tool is a classic Hoabinhian artifact. In Thailand with the Hoabinhian pebble tools the occurrence of flakes and incipient blades is a marked feature. With radiocarbon dates available from various sites in Vietnam, Thailand, Laos, Cambodia, Myanmar it is clear that the early stage of Hoabinhian belong to the late Pleistocene stage. The occurrence of flaked artifacts with the short axes and Sumatraliths has also been reported. In the cultural level I of Spirit Cave in Northern Thailand retouched and utilized flake category is by far the largest and most interesting group of artifacts (Gorman 1970: 103). Such an association was also reported from the Sai Yok cave of Western Thailand dated to the early Holocene (van Heekeren and Count Eigil Knuth 1967: 23-38). Recent discoveries at the Lang Rongrien and Moh Khiew in southern Thailand has shown that a distinctly non-Hoabinhian flakes tool industry existed in southern Thailand about 30,000 years ago. The fact that a somewhat similar industry, with dates in the 20,000 B.P. range, is now recognised in Vietnam (at Nguom and Mieng Hosee Ha) suggest that medium-sized thin tools made on flakes may have been quite widespread during the later Pleistocene in Southeast Asia. Majority of these flakes and blades are unretouched and amorphous in shape. But they all showed indications of utilisation. These give credence to the postulate that the lithic flake tools in Southeast Asia were complemented by a non-lithic and, therefore, perishable material such as bamboo and wood (Ronquillo 1981: 10).

The bifaces made on dolerite slabs have parallels within the Palaeolithic context of India. The presence of this trait in the study area indicates diffusion. But it is even possible that the technique was an indigenous development.

One of the distinguishing characteristics of the lithic assemblages of Garo Hills is the frequent occurrence of flakes with a concave edge. These have been found in different sizes with the Neolithic celts and also they occur in the typical flake-blade assemblage. These concave edges are very convenient tools for smoothening wood or bamboo. The metal knives used by the inhabitants of the area today also have concave edges, which they use for chopping, slicing bamboo into fine strips of various sizes, smoothening rough wood or sharp edges of bamboo etc. Prolific occurrence of this type of tools clearly indicates heavy bamboo and woodworking. This type of concave damage patterns was also noted in the lithic tools of Spirit Cave. Gorman suggested that it indicated working of small diameter wooden or bamboo shafts (Gorman 1970: 102).

The short axes occur in all the three assemblages. With the celt assemblage fully ground and polished short axes and partially ground short axes are found while with the bifaces and the flake-blade assemblage chipped short axes were found. Certain specific adaptability conditions must have influenced the re-occurrence of this type which no other tool type could fulfil. It is a component of the Hoabinhian tool kit and is often referred as a cutting tool. In the flake blade assemblage and also within the bifaces of the Ganol-Rongram valley no heavy duty cutting tool is present. Mainly scrapers and choppers constitute the assemblage. The short axes must have served the purpose. In the ground and polished tool kit the short axes are much bigger and stronger then the flat celts which must have been advantageous for certain purpose.

An attempt has been made to reconstruct the reduction sequence of the three assemblages. The specific techniques of reduction seem to depend on the size and shape of the raw material. As only one type of raw material was available there was not much choice. A tendency to shape the tool by minimum flaking is obvious. The prepared core technique is unique of the region. The attempt to produce two varieties of flakes from a single core is noteworthy. The flakes are usually flat in character with a subdued bulb. Also the flakes removed on the short axes are shallow. This indicates a controlled flaking technique. But the type of hammers used is hard to determine. Round granite pebbles found in the sites could have been used as hammers. These pieces are procured from particular areas which indicates they must have been brought to the site for some specific purpose.

In the absence of absolute dates from the area the dating remains arbitrary. On the basis of stratigraphy it is clear that the flake-blade assemblage, the bifaces and the pebble tools belong to the Pleistocene period. From the geological evidence on the evolution of the landscape it is ascertained that the colluvial deposits started forming from the Middle Pleistocene period. On this basis the assemblages found within the colluvium can be dated to the late/terminal Pleistocene period. The celt assemblage in the area occurs within the yellowish brown alluvium which is Holocene in origin. Earlier workers on the basis of typology have divided the Neolithic into two phases. The early phase without shouldered celts was relatively dated to 5000 B.C and the later phase with shouldered celts was dated to 2000 B.C. Without its division into any phases this assemblage can be dated to the middle part of the Holocene period.

SUBSISTENCE AND ASSOCIATED SETTLEMENT PATTERN: AN ETHNO-ARCHAEOLOGICAL ANALYSIS

Theorists have often stated that in the humid tropics the bulk of the material culture of Hominids is of perishable materials that quickly disappear from archaeological record. Thus, archaeologists working in such climatic zones often have to deal with data in between which wide gaps are visible. Attempts are often made to find the missing links but the results of such attempts are rarely fruitful. These results have given birth to terms like 'cultural stagnation' or 'cultural retardation' (Movius 1948). Cultural conservatism of prehistoric stone technologies in Southeast Asia has been a topic of discussion for the prehistorians of the area. A typical account of the view, and, by implication the view that an ancient pebble tool tradition 'survived', with little change in Southeast Asia until late prehistoric times is given by Heekeren and Knuth: "As we look back in time as far as the Middle Pleistocene, a curious picture emerges. The lower Palaeolithic Southeast Asian chopper chopping-tool industry, which is of that age, as has been proved by investigations made in West Punjab and North India (Soanian), in Burma (Anyathian), in Malaya (Tampanian), in Java (Patjitanian), and in North China (Choukoutienian), seems to have survived with only minor changes and innovations not only throughout the entire Pleistocene period, but even into post- glacial times in many parts of the tropical zone of the Far East"(van Heekeren and Knuth 1967: 110). Hallam Movius in 1943 after investigating a number of archaeological localities in India, Southeast Asia and China identified a geographical boundary, now known as the Movius Line, extending through Northern India, that separates two long lasting Palaeolithic cultures (Pope 1989: 49-57). West of the line are found collection of tools with a high percentage of symmetrical and consistently proportioned handaxes, called the Acheulean tools and east of the line are found crudely made tools known as choppers and chopping tools. Both types of tools are attributed to our hominid ancestors but Acheulean tools have long been

regarded as more advanced than the more crudely made less standardized tools of the Far East. In 1948 he published his conclusion that the Far East was a region of 'cultural retardation'. For years this explanation was accepted and even, in the interpretations of later workers, taken as evidence of racial isolation and backwardness. But further research decried the notion of cultural retardation or cultural stagnation (Solheim II 1970: 153). One of the many explanations forwarded for the apparent technological conservatism in the lithic industries of humid tropical environment is that our view of the prehistoric tropical cultures is seriously skewed by the invisibility (because of the lack of organic preservation) of the most significant part of the material culture actually in use by the prehistoric peoples. In Southeast Asia, bamboo, liana, rattan, various reeds, and wood must have shaped the course of prehistoric technology for more then one million years (Pope 1989: 49-57) (Hutterer 1976: 225).

There is a general belief that life in the tropics is marked by reduced need for substantial shelter and protective clothing and abundance of produce of the land available at any time of the year makes food procurement an easy task. But things are not so simple due to the extremely fine-grained distribution of resources. The term fine grained is used here to describe small patches of food resources, with wide gaps between two such patches in the thickly vegetated tropical forests with strong seasonal variation. This favours small social groups, high mobility, and the exploitation of a relatively large home range. In this condition the exploitative pattern cannot be specialized, but has to include a wide range of dietary items. This provides an explanation for two archaeological patterns generally noted about hunting and gathering assemblages from Southeast Asia: a pronounced broad spectrum exploitation pattern, as evidenced by faunal assemblages, and a generalized tool kit. The collection of a wide range of resources necessitates the use of a variety of specialized tools. This is especially true for the collection of animal protein. Variety of arrows and traps are often described in ethnographic reports. The evidence of generalized lithic assemblages from prehistoric hunting- gathering sites is in consistence with both continuing ethnographic pattern and ecological models, for the exploitation of fine grain environments. The need to manufacture a large variety of specialized extractive tools results in a corresponding need to economize in the energy expended in that process. That is, the energy invested in the procurement of raw material and the manufacture and curation of tools must be balanced against the energy gained through the use of these tools. Since any one of them may be used only occasionally and under special circumstances, energy investment has to be kept to a minimum. Utilizing widely available raw material, thus disposing of many problems of procurement and the need of extensive curation can do this. Such materials are the highly siliceous and lightweight bamboo, a variety of woody vines, and other tropical woody plants. The importance of these raw materials for early Southeast Asian hunting technologies has been postulated often. The manufacturing process calls for lithic tools with very limited requirements: sharp edges of certain configurations and sharp points. Such tools can be created at a moment's notice and from a variety of raw materials, thus further reducing outlay for procurement and maintenance. Both pebble tools and generalized "amorphous" flake tools fulfil most requirements of multipurpose manufacturing implements as postulated here. The basically conservative character of Southeast Asian lithic assemblages has been recognized and acknowledged by most archaeologists. The conservatism of the maintenance technology is primarily conditioned by ecological factors, and the extractive technology is far more flexible (Hutterer 1976: 225). The early Asians may have relied heavily on tools that they made from raw materials other than stone, and since these are seldom preserved at archaeological sites, we simply lack a balanced appreciation of their accomplishment. Thus, the absence of a

major portion of the cultural material in the archaeological record makes it look backward in physical development (Pope 1989: 49-57).

Almost a similar situation exists in Northeast India. In the Ganol-Rongram valley, the study area ground and polished tools are the only convincing evidence of a prehistoric agricultural society. These are specialised tools. Potsherds found with the tools provide us some additional data. The stone age archaeological record of the whole area consists of only lithic tools. These implements were probably made for procuring food as well as for building shelters. But no evidence have survived on the type of food procured and the type of shelters constructed. For the reconstruction of the material culture of the prehistoric inhabitants of the area the data in the form of the lithic tools is insufficient.

Besides the tools and potsherds no other evidence on house type, probable food processing techniques etc has survived. This makes proper reconstruction of the society difficult. It will not be wrong to say that the data is insufficient.

The huge amount of flake tools present has often been dubbed as debitage product or even as ecofacts at times (Ghosh 1977). This situation has arisen because of the peculiar nature of the tools. The parallel-sided flakes with a prominent positive bulb of percussion can be called blade like flakes but not blades. This is because the length of the flake is not twice its breadth. But the reconstruction of the technique for producing these flakes makes it clear that they were meant to be blade like flakes. Dolerite the raw material used and the only type of raw material available in the area was not suitable for making proper blades. The high percentage of simple flakes in the assemblage was also misleading. But as stated in the last chapter these are processing tools not tools by themselves. These tools have been always interpreted by keeping the mainland Indian lithic industries in the background. That is why the archaeological record of the Ganol-Rongram valley also gives an impression of cultural stagnation. Absence of associated finds like floral and faunal data, settlement data, made it difficult to understand the record. To give a proper meaning to the generalised tool kit we have to understand the processes, which operated to bring these assemblages into existence. These processes are the dynamics of the past cultural system and their material by-products, which form the archaeological record today (Binford 1980: 5).

The simple societies living today are often defined as remnants of past cultural systems. An ethnographic study of these simple societies can provide us reliable hints about the past cultural systems. Greater significance is attached to societies under ecological conditions, which approximate the conditions of the prehistoric culture under investigation. According to V Gordon Childe an analogy drawn from the same region or ecological province is likely to give most convincing conclusions. Thus, through ethnoarchaeological study of the living system, does the archaeologist stand the best chance of gaining sufficient understanding to begin the task of giving meaning to the archaeological record, in short, of developing tools or methods diagnosing patterned variability (Binford 1980: 5).

Ethnoarchaeological research investigates aspects of contemporary socio-cultural behaviour from an archaeological perspective; ethnoarchaeologist attempt to systematically define relationships between behaviour and material culture and to ascertain how certain features of observable behaviour may be reflected in remains which archaeologists may find. The utility of insights into past behaviour derived from observations of contemporary behaviour is greatest when they can be framed as hypothesis and tested. 'Ethnographic analogy' is the term used to define assumptions outlined above (Kramer 1979: 1-2). The theoretical basis of ethnoarchaeology is the use of analogies derived from present observations to aid interpretation of past events and processes. Archaeologists make observations in contemporary societies to provide themselves with as many and as varied interpretive hypothesis as possible to help understand archaeological remains. The

Garos, an Indo-Mongoloid ethnic group speaking a Tibeto-Burman dialect are the present inhabitants of the Ganol-Rongram valley. They are shifting cultivators and the ancient techniques of bark cloth making, fishing by poisoning is still practised by them. Through observations made on the Garo society it can be hypothetically stated that the prehistoric inhabitants of the area also relied heavily on tools made from raw materials besides stone. Due to lack of preservation these objects are absent in the archaeological record.

We can give a proper meaning to this record if we can fill up the gaps and understand the processes that transform the record from the present to the past. All forms of cultural behaviour, which existed in the past, are not available for observation today. Through analogical reasoning we can attempt to get near the truth. Analogy is generally equated with making inferences about non- observed behaviour by reference to relevant observed behaviour. This usually involves the incorporation of non-archaeological data sources, such as ethnography and ethnohistory, into analogies and the use of inductive inferences "to interpret" the archaeological data. Frequently such a mode of interpretation is considered limited and limiting rather than productive (Charlton 1981: 132).

Through field observations it has been ascertained that in the study area ethnology and archaeology overlaps. For example, the rubber stone frequently found in the archaeological context is also a household implement of the present inhabitants. It is the study of this very special corpus of data within the living community, which holds the most fruitful promise for analogy in archaeological interpretations.

The distribution of archaeological materials is almost always a product of many years and even generations of use. It reflects not an articulation of a "typical seasonal round" with permanent landscape features but rather many years of the establishment and abandonment of residential occupation on a landscape some of whose features altered over time in response to previous use. From the archaeological record of the study area it is almost certain that people has never abandoned the basin from the time it has been first inhabited. As stated in the previous chapter subsistence pattern seems to have changed from hunting gathering to shifting cultivation. In a very minor scale plough cultivation has also started very recently. These changes have modified the landscape and the signatures of previous use are likely to be erased. Tracing of these signatures of inhabitants of different periods is one of the major challenges for the ethnoarchaeologists working in the area.

The role of depositional and post-depositional processes with regard to evidence of settlement pattern and artifact distribution is to be identified to give meaning to the archaeological record. Then analogies between the archaeological past and the present can be framed with a clear understanding of how material remains of the present pass on to the archaeological record. Certain behaviour of man on the landscape leaves certain type of material residues. If we intend to investigate the relationship between static's or material residues and dynamics or behaviour, we must be able to observe both aspects simultaneously; and the only place we can observe dynamics is in the modern world (Binford 1983: 23, 49). Also while the range of activities carried out by ethnographically documented societies is very large, and the ways of characterizing these activities larger still, only a limited range of activities will contribute directly to the formation of the archaeological record, either by generating debris or by modifying the natural land surface. Debri-generating behaviours may be grouped into categories:

(a) procurement, or the gathering, hunting, harvesting or collecting of natural or cultivated materials for immediate or later consumption or manufacturing.

(b) processing of food into ready- to-eat states by such activities such as butchering, peeling, cracking of shells, roasting etc.

(c) manufacturing or the processing of nonfood items into artifacts or other culturally significant items or modified surfaces.

(d) construction and abandonment of shelters. During any of these four debris-generating behaviours, objects may be left at the locus of the activity through discard, loss abandonment, or deliberate burial. Objects removed from the activity context may either be destined for further use, or for secondary disposal (Brooks and Yellen 1987: 70).

These four categories of debri generating behaviour of the Garo society is discussed below to understand the relationship between the statics or material residue and dynamics or behaviour. Analogic reasoning concerning the relationship between the form and distribution of items of material culture and socio-cultural behaviour patterns based on certain hypothesis might help us to give a meaning to the otherwise conservative, less understood archaeological record of the area.

Settlement pattern and associated debris

Gordon Willey in 1953 defined the term 'settlement pattern' ... as the way in which man disposed himself over the landscape on which he lived. It refers to dwellings and to the nature and disposition of other buildings pertaining to community life. These settlements reflect the natural environment, the level of technology on which the builders operated the various institutions of social interaction and control, which the culture maintained. Because settlement patterns are, to large extent, directly shaped by widely held culture needs, they offer a strategic starting point for the functional interpretation of archaeological cultures (Chang 1972: 1-2). Mainly human geographers and ethnographers study settlement patterns of living peoples. In archaeology it is defined as the archaeological methodology in which settlement components, considered as loci of past activities, serve as the primary units for classification (Chang 1972: 7). These points of past activities are the sites, which are ruins of settlements and remains of past activities that accumulated during a certain period of time.

The Garos, are the linguistic kindred of other speakers of the languages of the Bodo group of the Tibeto-Burman family spread all over Assam. By Lexico-Statistic dating method the linguists have dated the separation of the Garo language from the original Bodo speech to about 2,000 years ago. According to their folklore they are supposed to have migrated from Tibet in search of better lands and after wandering in the Brahmaputra valley settled down in the Garo hills. It is generally accepted that they have migrated to the area though there is no definite proof of such movements.

Traditional Garo villages, with closely clustered houses are usually situated near some stream or waterfall. There is no concept of private ownership of property. The clans and the village own land. Thus, there is no perfect measurement of homestead land. A family can use as much land is necessary and is available. The Garo family consists of the parents, their unmarried children and the spouse and children of the youngest daughter if she is married. They build their houses with easily available forests products like bamboo, wood, thatch and cane. Their entire house is built on a bamboo platform called *machang*. The houses of a village can be divided into three categories:

(1) The dwelling house (*dongchakani nok*) (Plate 26)

(2) The granary (*jam nok*)

(3) The bachelors dormitory (*nokpante*) or the village meeting house (*bandasal*).

Materials used for the construction of all three categories are, round posts with clefts on top, split bamboo for floor and walls, whole bamboo for rafters and the frame for the roof, and thatch for the roof. Small strips of bamboo are used for tying. Nowadays thatch is scarce in the vicinity, so as a substitute, bamboo leaves tied in bundles are often used. The floor is constructed with round timber and whole bamboo, over which the split bamboo is spread. This bamboo is fixed to the frame with bamboo or cane strips. The same method is used for the construction of walls as well. The roof is constructed with whole bamboo, over which bundles of thatch or bamboo leaves are laid layer over layer until the whole area is covered. The dwelling house has a rectangular ground plan, the dimensions of which range between twenty inches to fifty inches in breadth. It has a porch in the front end, which is on the ground level. The main floor consists of a big hall, a portion of which is walled. In the middle of the room is the common fireplace. It is made of three stones placed in a triangular manner on a base of beaten earth put over the split bamboo floor. The next room of the house is known as *dun*, which is the sleeping room for the family. Towards the end of the house almost one-fourth or one-third of the entire length of the house is kept free and open. This is used to sun paddy, stocking of crops in winter etc. Only one door is kept for entrance and exit. Fowls are kept in one corner of the house while pigs are kept below the bamboo platform.

Plate 26: A Traditional Garo House

Houses are also built on treetops and are called *boring* (Plate 27). The average size of these houses is ten or eight feet in length and eight or six feet in breadth. But some are smaller then this size also. These are built in the agricultural fields to guard the crop. These are also used for sleeping purpose in areas where wild animals abound.

The granary built a little away from the dwelling house is also constructed in the same process and with the same kind of materials. It has a square ground plan, roughly eight inch in length and eight inch in breadth.

Bachelor's dormitory or *nokpante* is a very big house built of wood, bamboo, thatch and cane. Sometimes a *nokpante* is twenty feet high and eighty to ninety feet long. It is built on a bamboo platform that is six feet to ten feet in height from the ground and its walls are neatly woven. Almost half the length of the house is kept open while the other half in enclosed with bamboo mats of sufficiently polished works. There is a front door and a back door. A big log of wood with steps cut into it is used as the ladder. Carvings and paintings are also worked into the front posts of the *nokpante*. There are big wooden posts. Heads and tusks of pigs slaughtered for village or community feast are sometimes hung from the beams. Inside the house on the bamboo platform a rectangular hearth is constructed. Certain public property like feathers of fowls, horns of cattle and drums and gongs are kept in the *nokpante*. These dormitories also serve as meeting places for the village elders.

In present times bachelor dormitories are rarely seen. Also the villages no more consists of closely clustered houses. The houses are scattered and constructed near the roads built in recent years by the government. Only at times families belonging to the same lineage live in closely clustered houses. But the raw material used for construction is same and also the house type has not changed. Also the preference for places with perennial supply of water still exists and therefore it is common to find the houses clustered around such a source.

During the cultivating season the whole family shifts to the field house made in the plot cleared for cultivation. This is a miniature form of the main house in the village. Often a very simple single room house is built and a tree house is built nearby which is used for sleeping. In this house the family resides for a period of six to seven months starting from April to October. While they do not dismantle their original house in the village the inhabitants dismantle the field house when they leave the field after the harvest. When they shift from their village to the field house they carry with them the necessary utensils, furniture etc. which they bring back. All movable goods in a Garo household can be divided into three heads (Sangma 1991: 304-312). A list is provided below:

Plate 27: A Tree House or Borang

Agricultural implements (Plate 28)

1) *Atte*: This is a versatile bush knife with a curved iron blade that is in average seventy centimetres long. It is hafted into a bamboo or wooden handle and is mainly used for clearing the jungle and also for cutting, slicing, chipping etc. For a Garo male residing in the village it is like an ornament. They carry it constantly. It is a multipurpose tool.

2) *Gitchi*: This is a type of scraper made of an iron blade that is approximately ten to fifteen centimetres. It has a wide cutting edge and a perforation in the opposite end through which a bamboo's root or wood is fixed to work as a handle. It is used to scrape the ground and remove weeds. It is also at times used to plant tubers. It is interesting to note that the neolithic stone axes found in the area are called *Goira Gitchi* by the Garos. *Goira* in their dialect means God.

3) *Jakenbrak*: It is a rake made of bamboo about three to four feet long. At one end it is split like fingers and is woven by bamboo

strings. It is used for removal of dry roots and weeds from the cultivation field.

4) *Mattha*: This is the digging stick. It is made of a branch of a tree the maximum diameter of which do not exceed ten centimetres. The branch is dressed and one end is made pointed. It is a tool that is found mainly in the field house. It is discarded after use in the field and scarcely brought back to the main settlement.

Katchi or sickle, *Attema* or big iron knife and *Rua* or Axe made of iron are certain implements used by the Garos these days. These implements resemble the sickle, knife and axe used by people all over the world. In the lithic assemblage of Garo Hills axes made by ground and polishing technique are very common, while crudely shaped knife and sickle are also found. So, there seems to be transition from lithic to metal tools though there are no deposits to acquire the raw material for making the metal tools locally. These implements are prized and preserved well by the Gars and they carry it to and from the main house to the field house and again back.

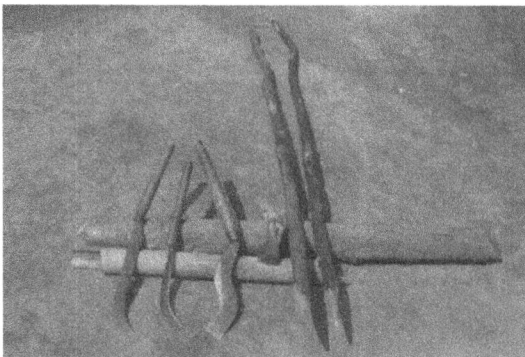

Plate 28: Implements used for Jhum Cultivation

Household utensils (Plate 29)

5) *Me'dik*: It is an earthen pot used for cooking rice. It has a rounded bottom with a constricted neck and wide mouth. The size of this earthen pot varies.

6) *Sam'dik*: It is also a wide mouthed earthen pot used for cooking, mainly for making other things besides rice. The size depends on the choice of the user.

7) *Dikka*: It is a big earthen pot about three to four feet long, with a globular body and is used to brew rice beer.

8) *Janchi*: This is a strainer made out of bamboo strings. This strainer is forced down to the fermented rice and water. The liquor then percolates into the strainer, from which it is ladled out with an empty gourd.

9) *Me'gol*: It is a deep ladle made of bamboo specifically used to stir rice. The size depends on the owner's choice.

10) *Brak*: It is a shallow ladle made of bamboo that is used for stirring curry and also for distributing curry. Here too the size varies according to necessity.

11) *Kabe*: It is a bamboo tube four to six feet long used for carrying drinking water from the source to the house. The inner knots are removed for convenience.

12) *Bek*: These are dried bitter gourds that are used as flask or water bottles. It has a globular body and a narrow neck and a beaded top in which they make a hole. Through this hole they pour out the liquid.

13) *Rimol*: It is a pestle carved out of a tree or a branch of a tree. It is in average four feet long and about three- inch in diameter.

14) *Sa'sam*: It is a mortar carved out of a big piece of log with a depression in the center.

15) *Am*: This is a bamboo mat that is about five feet long and three feet broad. It is used for drying paddy.

16) *Ruan*: It is a winnowing tray made of bamboo that is found in two shapes. One is circular with an average diameter of forty centimetre and the other is an elongated half circle in shape. The average length varies between fifteen to thirty centimetres. It is woven with thin strips of bamboo.

17) *Gitchera*: It is a sieve made of thinned pieces of bamboo the diameter of which is same as a winnowing tray. It is used mainly for separating the rice from the chaff.

18) *Kera*: It is a basket made out of thin flat pieces of bamboo. It is conical in shape but

has a flat bottom. The average height is between half a meter or less then that and the diameter is twenty-five centimetres. It is used in the house for storing betel nut, vegetables etc. for daily use.

19) *Kokcheng*: It is bamboo basket woven with thin flat pieces of bamboo the average height of which exceeds one meter. The average diameter is fourty centimetres. It is used for carrying firewood, cotton from the field, food to the field, wild leaves, tubers from the jungle, goods to be sold or bought from the market etc. It is carried on the back with the help of a flat strap that hangs from the head. It serves the purpose of a ladies purse or a portfolio bag.

Plate 29: A Gourd Pitcher used for Storage of Grain

Furniture

Traditional Garo houses contain limited furniture. The bamboo floor called *Gnashing* serve the purpose of both bed and chairs. At times a bamboo or cane mat is used on the floor.

20) *Am'pok*: This is low stool hewn out of a piece of wood.

21) *Mora*: This is also a low stool but woven with thin strips of bamboo or cane.

Bamboo tubes, baskets, earthen pots hung from the roofs are used to store seeds, dry fish or meet and even valuables. These days in some houses plastic containers, plastic packets, boxes etc. are seen. Besides these, other household goods consist of the clothes they wear.

The traditional hunting weapons have almost vanished. Most of the people now use guns, which are again very few. The traditional hunting weapons consisted of bows and arrows and spear made of bamboo and cane. They are known as *Chri* and *Bra* and *Sel'u* respectively. They are no more in use and neither people make them. On being questioned about the matter they said that they have lost the expertise. Fishing is a very common activity and fishing by poisoning is the most common method used at present. Varieties of hooks and traps are also used. The musical instruments are housed in the village chief's house only or in the public meeting hall. All this objects are made of bamboo.

Settlement Shift

The rural Garos prefer to change their place of residence after every five or ten year. In the study area a family has stayed in a single house for fifteen years, which is the longest time period recorded. The shortest period recorded is three years. According to the informants they feel residing for long in the same area have many disadvantages like:

(1) The homestead area becomes unhygienic and polluted after a certain point of time after which shifting is necessary

(2) Natural resources around the area like firewood, wild tubers, berries etc, gets depleted after a point of time, the soil becomes infertile and the water becomes polluted. So, they should leave.

(3) Prolonged stay in a place encourages the growth of the population of rodents and insects populations, which makes the granaries unsafe.

(4) Regular maintenance of the house is very important and after a point of time the structure becomes weak. Thus, when they have to build a new house for which they usually select a new place, which may be in a different village or in the same neighbourhood.

Thus, three structure abandonment strategies can be seen:

(1) Planned seasonal abandonment/return anticipated.

(2) Planned seasonal abandonment/ return not anticipated

(3) Planned unseasonal abandonment/ return not anticipated.

Abandonment conjures up images of catastrophe, mass migration, and environmental crisis. Abandonment can occur at the level of the activity area, structure, settlement, or entire region (Cameron 1993: 3). In the Ganol- Rongram valley, activity areas are abandoned and no catastrophic reason can be cited for their abandonment. Within the valley movement is planned and activity area specific. Where abandonment is planned and gradual, variables such as anticipated return to the site or distance to the next new settlement will affect abandonment behaviour. Thus, when the Garos seasonally abandon the main house only the necessary movable goods are carried to the field house. The house structure remains intact together with the surplus goods or goods not required in the field house. This is the first abandonment strategy.

When abandonment is planned and no return anticipated usable artifacts might be removed. If the distance to the new settlement in not great, even, structures may be dismantled and building materials transported (Cameron 1993: 5). When the Garos leave the field houses they carry back the household goods and furniture's and also at times dismantle the house and carry parts of the structure to be used in their main house or as fuel. Broken pieces of glass bottles or mirrors, broken plastic utensils or other such refuse which constitute a very

minor percentage of their household goods at present times, are collected and buried under a tree or in some lesser used corner of the area. Care is taken in their disposal because after some years this patch of land will be used for cultivation. This is the second abandonment strategy identified in the study area (Plates 30 & 31).

Plate 30: Field house under construction

Plate 31: After the field house is abandoned

When the main house is abandoned for a new one the whole structure is dismantled. All movable goods are carried away and the unmovable parts are dismantled. For sometime the abandoned patch of land will be identifiable on the basis of the posthole marks, sparse vegetation etc. But after a few couple of years the posthole marks completely disappear and vegetation thickens. After fifty years or so it becomes difficult for the owner to identify the exact location. During the period of residence broken or worn out artifacts are disposed, which get buried and passes into the archaeological record. Also the debitage formed in the process of making the artifacts gets buried around the homestead land. At times artifacts also slip into a buried context by accident. Gradually this abandoned piece of land is covered by thick vegetation. After a few years this plot is used for cultivation. This movement can be called planned unseasonal abandonment with no return anticipated. This is the third strategy.

These three strategies also speak of the depositional processes concerning structures, which are important for predicting what is likely to happen to dwellings after abandonment. The post-depositional processes eradicate a major part of the data, leaving traces of settlement in the form of artifact scatters.

Of the twenty-one household goods listed above only two objects, the hoe and the axe is made of metal. The rest of the objects are made of bamboo, cane and clay. This means that ninety percent of the material culture consists of objects made of organic material and clay. Preservation of these objects in a tropical humid climate is very poor. In fact a winnowing tray, a ladle or a rake used in the household survives maximum for five years. Longevity of a house built with bamboo is approximately ten years with maintenance. Thus, there is no scope of these objects passing on to the archaeological record.

Scattered dwelling structures, built on platforms, each near a source of clean portable water with no specific boundaries between two households are the characteristic features of the settlement pattern of a contemporary Garo village. Tree houses and field houses are constructed in the agricultural field during the cultivating season. Seasonal shift from the main house to the field house is a regular feature. There are also planned unseasonal shifts of the whole household after a few years. The raw materials used for building the house and also other material objects necessary in daily life are bamboo, cane and clay. Metal is rarely used. So, potential archaeological traces are likely to be limited.

Burial and preservation of the debris is important for the formation of the archaeological record. Besides the material objects there is also very less chance of the preservation of food refuse, animal bones etc. The contextual milieu (e.g. environmental, technological, socio- cultural factors) within which site abandonment takes place contains the factors conditioning abandonment processes (Tomka and

Stevenson 1993: 191). The environmental and technological contextual milieu in the Ganol-Rongram valley has conditioned the abandonment processes in a pattern that the identification of past activity areas depends on the ten percent of the material culture likely to be preserved. This ten percent besides helping to identify the activity areas does not show any further traces of settlement.

Ethnoarchaeological studies select contemporary societies for study on the basis of the reformulated general analogy in which they posses some similarities in subsistence strategy and environment to the archaeological cultures of concern. According to J.G.D. Clark the archaeologists should restrict the field of analogy to societies at a common level of subsistence and should attach greater significance to analogies drawn from societies existing under ecological conditions which approximate those reconstructed for the prehistoric culture under investigation than those adapted to markedly different environments.

The abandonment strategies, the depositional and post-depositional processes identified above can be true for societies practicing shifting cultivation under similar ecological conditions. Thus, inferences made about the archaeological record on the basis of these strategies and processes will only be true for the assemblages of lithic tools that can be considered part of an economy based on shifting cultivation. These tools are ground and polished hoe and axe besides other flake tools found in the same context. Pottery have also been recovered from the site of Gawak Abri. This is a strong evidence supporting habitation in the area. The contemporary Garos do not make pottery but they use pots which they buy from the market. The list of household goods produced above contain the names of varieties of pots and their uses. But these are specifically household goods which are discarded most often in a broken state. Ethnographic observations revealed that broken pots are kept just outside the house under the platform or *Machang*, under some tree or any other lesser used spot. Thus, Gawak Abri must have been used as a homestead land. On the basis of the above observations hypothetically we can say that those sites and layers with ground and polished axes and hoes and pottery is formed by the process of the third abandonment strategy identified above. On these basis it can be said that these were the main points of residences.

There are sites and layers in the Ganol-Rongram valley in which no polished and ground tools have been found. These assemblages of tools typologically and also geologically belong to a different context. These sites are found in close proximity to a dolerite dyke exposure, which is the prime source of raw material and to a source of water. In the two hundred square kilometre study area starting from the source of Ganol to the confluence of the Ganol and its tributary the Rongram, as noted earlier there are no caves or rock shelter that could have provided shelter to the inhabitants. As explained in the previous chapter these sites contain finished tools, flakes, cores, debitage and chips. On the basis of the contents these areas can be called factory sites. The finished tools consist of digging tools, varieties of scrapers, crude blades etc. It is a flake- blade assemblage. They typologically belong to an economy based on hunting and gathering. The Garos add a lot of wild food collected from the jungle in their normal diet. Especially during the cultivating season until the harvesting of the first batch of early variety of paddy many rural Garos live completely on jackfruit, variety of tubers etc. collected from the jungle. But this habit of theirs reflects nothing on the settlement pattern. The collection is made by individual household on a daily basis. They carry the hoe or *gitchi* and the big iron knife or *dao*. The *gitchi* is used in digging and the knife for cutting or chopping and the bamboo basket or *kok* for carrying the collected items. But neither the archaeological record nor the ethnographic records, provides us with any data regarding the settlement pattern of hunters or gatherers. In general, activities involved with procurement such as hunting, gathering, or raw material collecting leave behind little or no debris, except to the extent that the necessary implements are manufactured on the spot. The distribution of activities in space,

however, suggests that gathering events, which tend to be widely dispersed, leave little or no concentration of debri or modification in the landscape. Raw material procurement such as stone quarrying and artifact manufacturing, however, are extremely localized in space and leave concentrations of debris and land modification (Brooks and Yellen 1987: 77). Thus, the buried or on surface lithic scatters must have been spots of raw material procurement and artifact manufacturing. All other evidences have been deleted which compels us to state that these settlers also constructed their shelters, a basic necessity of human beings with the locally available organic materials.

Conclusions drawn from the above analysis can be summarised as follows:

(1)   The sites with the ground and polished tools were the actual dwelling spots of the inhabitants.

(2)   The sites with the flake-blade tools are factory sites that might have been also used as residences.

(3)   Thatch for the roof, bamboo for the walls and floors and naturally obtained raw material have been used by settlers of all times for constructing houses and making household goods.

Subsistence activities and associated debri

The Garos are agriculturists. They practice shifting cultivation in the hills and also wet cultivation in the narrow valleys. The method as practised in the Garo hills is very simple. A plot, covered with jungle is cleared in the dry months, just before the monsoon starts. It is allowed to dry for a month or two. Just before the rains are expected, the plot is fired, and on the ash covered burnt soil seeds of verious cereals and plants are sown, dibbled or planted. After this the plants are constantly kept free from unwanted weeds. Crops become ready for harvest one after another in regular intervals. Occasionally such a plot is utilized for a variety of crops for a couple of years and then it is abandoned until it grows sufficient number of vegetation to be cut down and burnt (Plates 32, 33, 34, 35 , 36, 37, 38 and 39).

Plate 32: Jhum field cleared for cultivation

Plate 33: Sowing

Plate 34: Saplings of paddy

Plate 35: Jhum field from a distance

Plate 36: Field just before weeding

Plate 37: After weeding is completed

Plate 38: Ginger and Yam Plantation

Plate 39: Tapioca and Millet

There is no historical evidence about the origin of this method of cultivation among the Garos. It can be presumed that the Garos are practising this method of cultivation since these hills were inhabited by them. In Garo folklore it is mentioned that in the olden days, human beings cleared shifting plots but did not produce cereals. They used to plant cereals and other such roots. The God of wind, in collaboration with the god of hail and storm shook off the grains from the celestial tree. The seeds of different grains were then picked up and sown by the ancestress of the bird known as *do'mik*. From her the supreme God of celestial region obtained the seeds of rice and planted those in his own fields. Taking pity on the human beings, who in those days were living on grainless diet, he gave man the seeds with instruction that before every harvest a portion of the first seeds are to be kept aside for him. In this way there are innumerable folklores which explain the introduction of agriculture and cereals into the Garo land. In another folklore different crops are assigned to be cultivated by different sub- tribes of the Garo. However, at present we do not find such crops confined to particular areas or groups of people or sub tribes of Garos only. It is risky to make a generalization basing on this folk tales; but all this very clearly point out that shifting cultivation is very closely associated with the life of the Garo since very early times, and in early days it was the only method of raising crops known to them (Majumdar 1956; 1975).

The method of shifting cultivation and the crops grown is uniform in different areas of the district. Each Garo village has an area within which that particular village confines its shifting cultivation. This area is earmarked particularly for a village and it is called an *a'dok*. Within this boundary village elders allot individual families thir share of land. These plot of land is known as *a'king*. The villagers confine their cultivation within their *a'dok* within which they move in a cycle. Thus, the villagers know which area will be cultivated which year and which area was cultivated before how many years, and when will it be cultivated again. Land is a common property of the village. Once the plot is abandoned after one or two years of cultivation the land again reverts to communal ownership.

The selection of plots is made sometime in the last part of December. On the day of selection and allocation of plots each year each head of household clears a token patch. Usually clearing of the plot isdone by the males. The scrub growth is cut down is cut down, but big trees are not felled. Branches of these are chopped of, so that the whole plot gets good sunlight. The plots are fired on a day fixed by the common consent of the villagers. Common consent for firing the plots is required for two reasons: first, it is the duty of the villagers to see that the fire does not get out of control and spread to the plots of the other neighbouring villages, because firing is done during the dry months and as strong winds blow during that time, the danger of the fire spreading to the neighbouring areas always remains: second villagers are to get themselves ready for the *galmak* festival which is held immediately after firing the plots. The plot after being burnt is ready for sowing seeds usually in the middle of March. Seeds and plants are planted in different ways for different crops and methods vary in different areas. The main methods are stated below:

1. *Ge'a*: A hole is dug with the hoe(*gitchi*) and the root or head of the plant is planted in the hole and afterwards covered up with soil.

2. *Sika*: The dibble(*matta*) is thrust into the ground to make a hole where two or three seeds are put and covered up with soil.

3. *Baka*: Seeds are first broadcast and then the soil is lightly hoed, so that the seeds become nicely embeded in the soil.
4. *Sata*: This is the method of simple braosdcasting. All seeds to be sown are first mixed and then broadcasted.

Planting and sowing of seeds is mainly a job done by the females. Immediately after burning the fields, males get busy in constructing the field house. Before the rains come that is by mid April sowing is completed.A variety of crops are planted in one field but in a very well planned manner. Crops like paddy, ginger, yam etc, are grown in exclusive patches. Seeds of cimbers and creepers of different varieties of gourd are planted at regular intervals so that each plant gets enough space to spread horizontally. Tapiocca, maize and such other crops with a bushy plant is planted in a regular line along the boundary of the patches of crops. Trunks of very big trees the branches of which has been chopped are used as support for varieties of beans. Small patches of medicinal herbs, plantains etc. is often seen. The first weeding is done just after the seeds sprout up. For weeding, the soil is slightly loosened with the hoe, taking care not to damage the growing plants, and after this unwanted weeds are pulled out with hand. Plants are constantly kept free of weeds. But the second major weeding has to be done when the plants are frimly rooted. Harvesting starts with the ripening of early varieties of millet in the last part of August. The next crop harvested is rice. After the rice harvest long weeds are uprooted by pulling with the hand. This takes place in the month of October, when the rainy season comes to an end. After this the rice stalks and other unwanted plants are cut with a sickle, so that cotton plants can grow freely. Harvesting continues till the end of December.

The time schedule for harvesting crops from the field is :

Crops	Months
Millet (early variety)	August
Paddy (early variety)	August
Millet (late variety)	August
Melons/gourds	September
Brinjal/chilli, Paddy	October
Manioc/yams	November
Deccan hemp, Ginger, Arum, Beans, Sesame and Similar seeds	December
Cotton, Lac, Paddy (late variety)	January

There are also different methods of harvesting. Millet and cotton are harvested by hand. Sesame and such other plants are allowed to fall in a big basket after bending and jerking the plant over it. Paddy is harvested in two ways. Some of them milk the ears while the a recently they have started using sickle with which they reap the ear. All the principal crops like rice, different cereals etc are transferred to the granaries in the village.

Driving away wild animals like elephants,birds etc is another major activity during the period the crop is ripe in the field. In some areas the same plot is used for cultivation in the second year also. After harvesting all the crops the dried up plants are cleared and the debri is piled up in heaps all over the plot. These small heaps are burnt, the ashes of which add to the fertility of the soil. In most of the areas plots in the second year are used only for rice cultivation. But vegetables like brinjal, chilli is also occasionally cultivated while some allow all crops to grow for the second year also.

The field after one or two years of cultivation is left fallow for eight to ten years in present times. Earlier the cycle was much longer. The forest rejuvenates in these fields and the fertility of the soil is revitalised.

For shifting cultivation only a few very simple implements are used. These have been listed and described above.

The general agricultural calendar of the Garo who practice shifting cultivation as their main occupation show that their agricultural activities keep them busy throughout the year. All their main festivals are connected with the different activities in the agricultural field. Every member of the household male or female, young or old has a role to play .

The household is the main working unit in the shifting plots. In the plot they construct a hut smaller in size then the original house in the village but enough to hold the family if necessary and also a tree house. During the sowing and weeding season they use this hut only for resting purpose during the day. But sometimes when the crop is ripe to protect it from wild animals the whole household is temporarily shifted there and they also use this hut to store the harvested crop which is eventually shifted to the main household in the village. The products usually last them a whole year though in certain difficult years if the crop is bad they resort to food gathering. Sometimes heavy rains when the crop is ripe spoil the crop and in recent times wild elephants have also started causing damage. Otherwise the yield is very high. In recent years Garo hills have started to produce very high quality cotton, ginger, pineapple and chillies. Money economy has entered the region very recently though traditional weekly markets in certain areas have a very long history. In the villages barter is the most common method still for acquiring items of necessity. But villagers have developed taste for plastic items etc. sold by traders from outside in the weekly markets for which money has become a necessity which they try to acquire by selling their agricultural products.

The Garos have been always self sufficient in food. Their agricultural products are highly prized by the plains people. By selling this products in the weekly markets they obtain the other bare necessities like oil, which they rarely use, clothes medicines etc.

The spatial organization of activities in the ethnographic or "systemic" context underlies the organization of debris in the archaeological context. But the complexity of variables determining the spatial organization of activities in any society, together with the wide range of factors affecting the relationship between activities and debris disposal, burial, or preservation makes it difficult to develop models which explain the relationship between the archaeological record and ethnographic or systemic rules and practices of activity area use (Brooks and Yellen 1987: 64). A comparative study of the agriculture implements from the ethnographic contexts and the ground and polished axes and hoes from the arcaheological context in Garo hills reveals a homogeneity in function. This conclusion is based on a study made on the edge wear patterns of the stone axes and hoes found in the arcaheological sites and iron hoe blades used by the people today. Observation made on the functional aspect of the iron and lithic tools on the basis of the edge wear patterns again reveal homogeneity. So, an inference can be made that the constraints the people of this area face today were more or less the same for the neolithic peoples as well and there exists a great deal of similarity in their subsistence pattern (Roy 1981: 219). Thus, the makers

and users of the lithic hoes and axes were in all probability shifting cultivators. Ethnographic data from different parts of the world shows that shifting agriculture might leave minimal archaeological traces (Orme 1981: 278). In the study area when a plot is abandoned after two years of cultivation hardly any debri is formed. The discarded digging sticks, possibly a broken overused hoe blade and occasionally parts of a bamboo fencing built around the field constitutes the debris. Of this except the hoe blade there is no chance of the other materials surviving and passing on to the archaeological record. The vegetation soon rejunvenates and within two years the it again becomes impenetrable. Tree litter forms a thick layer on the ground and this transforms into a humus layer within a span of five to six years. At present the jhum cycle is six to eight years. So, after eight years when the same plot is used for cultivation, crops are planted on the humus layer. Field observations have confirmed that on this humus layer no debris of the previous cultivation is visible. Only on the basis of the typology of the lithic tools and the ethnographic evidence it can be inferred that the lithic tool makers practised shifting cultivation.

As noted a few pages earlier besides the ground and polished agricultural tools, in the study area there is an assemblage of flake tools which is a hunter-gatherer tool kit. The Garos are all agriculturist, but they occasionally practice hunting, gathering and fishing also. Fishing is very common during the rainy season. Fishes are either smoked or dried for storing. Same is the case with meat. The most common animals hunted is the deer. The extra meat is usually smoked and preserved. Collection of wild food from the jungle is a regular activity. As noted in chapter two, three varieties of forests are present in the study area. These forests with abundant resources provide a lot of nutritous wild vegetables, tubers etc.which are regularly added to the diet of the local inhabitants. But most plants are perishable, and many when used as food leave little or no debri. Bones of animals and fish do get preserved but in a humid tropical climate long time preservation is not possible. Thereby except the lithic tools and the debitage produced during its manufacture no other evidences have survived in the archaeological record.

In the absence of an ethnographic example of a full time hunting- gathering economy in the study area it is hard to draw inferrences. Reconstruction of an economic pattern is not possible. It is even difficult to say they were collectors or foragers. This complexity of variables determining the spatial organization of activities in the society, together with the wide range of factors affecting the relationship between activities and preservation makes it difficult to develop a model which will explain the relationship between the archaeological record and ethnographic or systemic rules. Interpretation of the presence of this assemblage of tools is possible only on a typo-technological level.

Conclusion

An attempt has been made in the previous pages to reconstruct the dynamic processes that might have been responsible for creating the archaeological record in the study area. The list of agricultural implements, household goods clearly proves that the majority of the items were made from organic raw material like bamboo, cane and wood. Dwelling structures were completely made from organic materials. For making these objects the contemporary Garos use bush knives and hoes with iron blades which constitutes approximately ten percent of their material culture. Before iron was available to them stone was the easily available material from which effective sharp axe and hoe blades could be made. But unfortunately in the study area the only suitable rock available for making tools was dolerite, which is one of the hardest rock. It was profusely available and a simple flake would have one or more sharp edges which was enough for working on the organic raw materials. Making of specialised lithic tools was difficult because of the raw material and

also it was not necessary. All the specialised tools needed could be made from bamboo, wood or cane. A flake after use was rarely resharpened or retouched because with much less effort a new flake can be acquired. This explains the occurrence of the generalised tool kit. The specialised tools were probably made of organic material which has not survived. Thus, the simple flakes, blade like flakes constitute a minor percentage of the actual tool kit of the past inhabitants. They are part of a culture when specialised lithic tools were not necessary. Also bamboo tools are portable and highly efficient because of their light weight. For mobile hunter-gatherers a bamboo tool kit would be very convenient. But when people started cultivation they needed axes for felling the trees and hoes for cultivation. The ground and polished celts, which are specialised tools were made by the agriculturist. These were resharpened as they were made with considerable effort.

The presence of a stage called the "Lignic" in Southeast Asian prehistory had been proposed in a developmental scheme for the prehistory of Southeast Asia. Chronologically it was placed in the Upper Palaeolithic period with an unnamed flake tool tradition and wood, especially bamboo becoming an important raw material for making tools (Solheim II 1970: 153). A statement that " In Asia, a giant grass may have shaped the course of prehistoric technology for more than one million years" (Pope 1989: 49) explains the vital role played by bamboo in the ancient past of this region. But is hard to confirm the presence of a lignic stage because the objects probably has not been preserved. These statements and proposals have been based on observations made on the contemporary society. Existence of such a stage in the prehistory of Northeast India can be hypothetically stated based on the observations made on the contemporary Garo society.

73

CONCLUSION

Affinities that exist in the archaeological record of two different places generally indicate contact. In the historical period contact was established through trade, peaceful migration or conquest. In the prehistoric period it is usually through peaceful migrations. These migrations can be triggered by the exhaustion of resources, population pressure or a general tendency of humans to trudge into unknown lands in search of new or better resources. But without physical contacts similar culture probably can develop in two different places as an adaptation to a similar physiographical environment if culture is accepted as a durable material expression of an adaptation to an environment.

There is no scope for debate on the fact that cultural affinities exist between Southeast Asia and Northeast India. It is an undoubted fact that can be attributed partly to peaceful migration and partly to adaptation to a similar environment. Majority of the people in this part of India belong to the Indo-Mongoloid stock and speak different dialects belonging to the Tibeto-Burman family of languages. This region can be called the Southwestern boundary of the Mongoloid inhabited areas of the world which further extends westward along the Himalayas until it reaches Tibet. With population movement cultural traits also travel. Dispersal of the Mongoloid population to different areas of South, Southeast and North Asia is believed to have taken place during the final phase of the prehistoric period. During this period the first wave of Mongolians must have entered Northeast India carrying with them the technique of making pebble tools and amorphous flakes. Consequent migrations brought in the Tibeto-Burman and the Monkhmer language. Migration into the area continued till the 13th-14th century A.D. The last recorded group is the Ahoms who is believed to have migrated from Thailand. Various folktales of the region are based on these migrations and distance lands from where they come indicating movement of population.

Under these circumstances affinities in the archaeological record between the two areas is expected. For giving meaning to the archaeological record of the region a holistic approach was necessary for understanding the regional geomorphology, the post-depositional processes distinctive to the region together with the typology and technology of the tools.

The archaeological record of the Ganol and Rongram valleys consists of lithic artifacts and potsherds. These are found on surface, subsurface or in buried context. In this study an area with high artifact density is called a site and all other finds within a radius of one kilometre are identified as localities of that site in the study area. The drainage is dendritic and majority of the sites are within deposits created by first-order and second-order streams. Ten sites and their localities have been studied in detail. They are Gawak Abri, Didami. Rongram IB, Ida Bichik, Bibragiri, Missimagiri, Selbal Bichik, Mokbol Bichik II, Chitra Abri, Mokbol Bichik I. The sediments within which the lithic tools are found consist of coarse angular sand and silt. As the specific area under study is the upper and middle course of the river the coarse character of the sediments is expected. But the thickness of the deposits which range between 2 cm and 10 cm is intriguing. The probable geomorphological processes that resulted in the formation of these thick deposits are tectonics caused by the upliftment of the Himalayas during the Middle Pleistocene (Himalayan Orogeny 4), excessive soil stripping caused by drier climatic conditions during the 18,000 B.P. glacial maxima and reworking of these sediments in the subsequent periods resulting in the deposition of the much finer material or alluvium. These fertile colluvial-alluvial deposits capable of supporting a very rich plant life, including edible foods and organic raw material, ample hunting ground and gathering area and cultivating fields, presence of perennial sources of water, dolerite dykes and river pebbles for making tools and dry ground surface to be used as dwellings even during rainy season are some of the resources which has governed human behaviour in the area. Distribution of the archaeological record conforms to the distribution of these resources. Artifact density and distribution reflect the pattern of resource utilization.

The analysis of the setting of the sites with the ground and polished Neolithic celts indicates a clear choice of the Neolithic dwellers of the area. The availability of the alluvial deposits with gentle slopes, together with dolerite dyke exposures and a perennial source of water determined the location of these sites. On the basis of the tool typology it is inferred that the authors of the lithic assemblage of the sites situated in the uplands like Didami, Missimagiri and Bibragiri and at Mokbol Bichik were non-agriculturist. These sites are very close to the steep slopes and the highest contours of the Tura range of mountains. The settlers of these sites had access to three different topographical situations: a) considerable stretch of upland areas in the form of the Tura and Arbella mountains; b) the valley in between the two mountains; and c) the comparatively flat flood plain of the Ganol river further downstream. Ample resources were thus available to the inhabitants of the area in all the seasons as topographical variation in the area allowed growth of resources in particular patches during particular seasons. Thus, artifact density and distribution reflect the pattern of resource utilization and the regional structure of the archaeological record, operating through uniform processes, vary with topography.

As a variety of resources can be exploited from a single location residential mobility is reduced to minimum. The economic potential of different locations becomes increasingly stabilized. Particular areas are seasonally exploited. Correspondingly, the use made of certain places becomes increasingly repetitive. The Ganol and Rongram basins have never been abandoned by people. Continuous exposure of the landscape to occupation and exploitation of the same resources have increased the density of material and a blurring of the spatial patterns. Thus, it is extremely difficult to calculate the size of the home range on the basis of artifact distribution.

There is no considerable difference in the density of artifacts of two different sites and the home range boundaries often overlap. Missimagiri, Bibragiri and Didami are sites with high artifact density but the distance separating them is not enough for the exploitation of individual home ranges. The high density of artifacts in these sites maybe because of repetitive use. It is accumulation of repeated events which has created this archaeological record. The home range boundaries of the Neolithic sites are much clearer. In these sites too accumulation of the material can be attributed to repeated use. Overlapping can be attributed to the cultural behaviour of the people of shifting agricultural fields.

Various post-depositional factors have operated in the area disturbing the accumulated artefactual material. The upper layers of the Rongram IB site have been sliced down for the construction of a building, a locality of the site Gawak Abri, called Miching Grenchep is presently under use as homestead land etc. All these various activities have caused considerable lateral and vertical movements of artifacts in certain areas resulting in their modified distribution and frequency. As a result within the study area stray finds are often recorded but in the absence of proper context their use is limited. This can be identified as one of the limitation of the data. The post-depositional processes eradicated a major part of the data.

The local conditions favoured no choice of raw material for making tools. Square or rectangular blocks of dolerite in varying thickness were extracted from dykes and round or oval shaped river pebbles in different sizes were collected from the river bed. A study on the typology of the tools has indicated the presence of three varieties of assemblages. They are:

(i) the celt assemblage

(ii) the core tool assemblage and

(iii) the flake-blade tool assemblage.

Assemblage here is used to define a collection of tools sharing typo-technological features.

The celt assemblage consists of rectangular celts with square butts and lenticular cross-section, shouldered celts with curved and square shoulders, edge ground celts, chipped celts and waisted axe. These occur within the yellowish brown deposit. At places where this layer has been disturbed the artifacts lie exposed. But on the basis of the stratigraphy and typology of the tools this assemblage can be relatively dated to the mid-Holocene period.

In the Rongram IB site the second cultural layer consisting of pebble tools and bifaces made on blocks and the flake-blade assemblage together with the bifaces at Missimagiri, Bibragiri and Didami occur within the strong or reddish brown layer. Short axes also occur with the flake-assemblage in almost all the sites. The flakes vary in size and shape. The blade flakes constitutes a separate category. Cores found in association with these flakes have confirmed that these flakes were removed by the prepared core technique. But the notable aspect of these cores is that from a single core two varieties of flakes, both blade flakes and amorphous flakes were removed. Roughly cylindrical cores were also found. But the length of the blades removed from these cores was not twice its breadth though they had sharp parallel edges. This suggests an incipient blade manufacturing technique. They can be called short blades. Retouching is rare to nil on these flakes for which they are referred in this study as probably utilised flakes. The amorphous character of the flakes which make these a generalized tool kit. Doubts have often been expressed about the utility of such tools and if it is worth classifying these tools as a separate assemblage. But their stratigraphic context clearly proves that this assemblage has an independent entity and the presence of the cores proves that they were manufactured. The size and shapes were intended to be what they are so. Regardless of their potential to achieve goals tools will not be manufactured unless they are considered necessary. They must have been employed by humans to perform some functions. It has often been postulated that the early Asians relied heavily on material made from highly siliceous and lightweight bamboo, a variety of woody vines, and other tropical woody plants. Majority of the specialised tools was made from these materials. The manufacturing process calls for lithic tools with very limited requirements: sharp edges of certain configurations and sharp points. The amorphous flakes of the Ganol and Rongram basins must have been processing tools. Due to lack of preservation the specialised tools are no more present in the archaeological record. As a result the data looks physically undeveloped. From an ethnographic account of the Garos, present inhabitants of the area it has been estimated that approximately ninety percent of their household goods are made of organic materials. The Garos belong to the Indo-Mongoloid racial group and they speak a dialect of the Tibeto-Burman family of languages. They are shifting cultivators and are regarded as one of the oldest ethnic group in the region. From an ethnoarchaeological analysis of the archaeological data it can be hypothetically stated that those sites and layers with ground and polished axes and hoes and pottery were the main locales of residence. But neither the archaeological record nor the ethnographic records, provides us with any data regarding the settlement pattern of hunters or gatherers or the people using the flake-blade assemblage. In general, activities connected with procurement such as hunting, gathering, or raw material collecting leave behind little or no debris. Raw material procurement such as stone quarrying and artifact manufacturing, however, are extremely localized in space and leave concentrations of debris and land modification. Thus, the buried or on surface lithic scatters must have been spots of raw material procurement and artifact manufacturing and probably points of residence. In the absence of caves or evidence of structural data it is perceived that the authors of both the assemblages built dwelling structures with locally available organic material like bamboo, wood etc.

A period called 'Lignic' with an unnamed flake tool tradition and wood and bamboo becoming an important raw material for making tools has been proposed in a developmental scheme for the prehistory of Southeast Asia. Chronologically it was placed in the Upper Palaeolithic period. It is difficult to prove the presence of this stage because the objects have not survived. But the type of artifacts and the absence of certain types of data in the archaeological record are convincing enough for proposing the existence of such a stage in the prehistory of Northeast India.

Cultural affinities between Stone Age cultures of Northeast India and Southeast Asia have been a topic of discussion for the archaeologists of both the regions from the beginning of the last century. But a coherent account of the relationship has still not emerged. Way back in 1949 E.C. Worman delving into the Neolithic problem of the India had stated that (I) Assam and Burma (now Myanmar) might have been the corridor through which celt making techniques entered India and (ii) the eastern half of India belonged to a fairly large east Asiatic area throughout which the evolution of post-Pleistocene cultures was more or less similar. These observations were based mainly on a study of celt typology within India. Similar opinions were expressed by H.D. Sankalia (1981), T.C. Sharma (1966), S.N. Rao (1980) and a host of other scholars working in the region. W.G. Solheim II (1969) while defining Southeast Asia stated that the western boundary of the region ends in eastern India. The similarities visible in the zoological and botanical life of the two regions have established that Northeast India and Southeast Asia belong to a common ecological zone. It is the only land route that connects India with Southeast Asia. All this has been taken as a strong factor for advocating the development of similar cultures in the two regions.

Within India the Neolithic culture of Northeast India has no parallel. Sporadic occurrence of tanged or shouldered celts, the distinctive trait of the Northeast Indian Neolithic, have been reported from Chota Nagpur and Dalbhum in Bihar, Baidyapur in Orissa, Lower Godavari in Andhra Pradesh and but none of these have been reported from stratified Neolithic context and with the associated cord marked pottery tradition. This typical eastern Asiatic Neolithic tradition and many other regional peculiarities have given the Northeast Indian Neolithic a distinctive character. It is established now that the Neolithic culture of Northeast India have strong affinities with the Eastern Asiatic Neolithic tradition. The Neolithic of the Ganol-Rongram valley is no exception. The lithic tools from this area consist of the ground and polished flat celts, the tanged or shouldered celts, the short axes and the chipped celts. A study of the lithic assemblages from certain sites of Western Thailand like Ban Kao, Sai Yok and Don Noi has shown that distinct similarities exist in typology. The chipped celts from Don Noi, Western Thailand and Rongram IB, Gawak Abri and Ida Bichik, Garo Hills are typologically similar. The celts from both the areas are roughly rectangular in shape with a curved working edge. Only one specimen found at Gawak Abri was triangular in shape, with a pointed butt end. Don Noi is a terrace of a first order stream which joins the Kwai Ai river. The site setting is similar to the sites from Ganol-Rongram basin which suggest similar adaptability conditions. There is a difference in size of the flat celts and also the tanged or shouldered celts. The celts from the Ganol-Rongram valley are smaller in size and also the shouldered celts have curvilinear or drooping shoulders. In average the celts from western Thailand are twice bigger in size length-wise than the celts from Garo hills. There is not much difference in breadth. This difference can be attributed to the difference in raw material. At Ban Kao, Sai Yok and Don Noi varieties of chert, chalcedony, slate etc are used while in the Ganol-Rongram valley dolerite is the only material available. As dolerite is a hard material and difficult to shape maybe the tools were used till their utility got reduced to the minimum. The size might have got reduced as a result of incessant use. The curvilinear shoulders were probably made by grinding. As the material is hard it will be difficult to cut square shoulders. By experiments and from ethnographic records it is known that square shoulders were cut and shaped by bamboo or wooden knives. Otherwise celts from both the areas have lenticular cross section and square butt end.

One major difference between the Neolithic culture of Ganol and Rongram basins and Southeast Asia is that cord marked pottery is absent in the sites of the study area. Cord marked pottery has been reported from other sites of Northeast India, like Daojali Hading, North Cachar Hills, Assam, Saru Taro, East Khasi Hills, Meghalaya, Parsi Parlo, East Siang, Arunachal Pradesh and from Manipur. At Gawak Abri potsherds found with the celts are plain. Two varieties of potsherds were found. One was very coarse and brittle while the second category had a thin slip which made it look comparatively fine. They were handmade with not very well levigated clay. No parallels have been noted till now from either Southeast Asia and Northeast Asia. It can be marked as a local development.

Two other lithic assemblages identified in the study area are the core tool assemblage and the flake-blade assemblage. The core tool assemblage is sub-divided into two parts, the pebble tools and the bifaces. The pebble tools include chopping tools, scrapers and short axes. Of these the short axes are typical Hoabinhian tools and they have no parallels in rest of India. These have been reported from the late Pleistocene-early Holocene sites of Vietnam, Thailand, Laos, Cambodia, Malaysia, Indonesia and all other areas with Hoabinhian assemblages. Assemblages with chopping tools prepared on river pebbles by removing a few flakes unifacially or bifacially on the working edge is also reported from all the Southeast Asian countries mentioned above. Radiometric dates ranging from 28,000 B.P. to 7,000 B.P. indicate that this trait survived all over Southeast Asia for a very long time. No radiometric dates are available from the study area. But this assemblage occur within the late/terminal Pleistocene deposit and is sealed by the Holocene deposit at the Rongram IB site. On this basis it can also be relatively dated to the terminal Pleistocene-early Holocene period.

At Rongram IB site the bifaces occur with the pebble tools while at Mokbol Bichik, Bibragiri and Didami they occur with the Flake blade assemblage. These bifaces are all made on blocks extracted from the dolerite dykes. In majority of them flakes are removed only from the edges. The rest of the tool, approximately 70% is left untouched. Chopping tools and knives are the most frequently occurring types. Almost all of them possess a truncated proximal end. Tools made on blocks have been reported from the Palaeolithic sites of India but no parallels exist in Southeast Asia. Thus, it is a trait of Indian Palaeolithic tradition which seem to have co-existed with the pebble tool and flake-blade assemblage in Ganol and Rongram valleys. This clearly indicates synthesis of two traditions in the region.

The flake-blade assemblage also shows strong Southeast Asian affinities. The flakes belonging to this assemblage do not posses well defined typological features and they are unretouched flakes. Utilized flake industries have been found *in situ* in datable context in western Palawan, Phillipines, Niah, Sarawak and in western, northern, northeastern and southern Thailand. These industries, unassociated or associated with choppers or chopping tools were in existence before and after 30,000 B.C in both Palawan and Niah Caves. The industries from north-western Thailand from the site of Spirit Cave have been dated between 6,600 B.C and 7,200B.C and earlier and as Mesolithic in Obluang. An irregular, amorphous flake assemblage has also been recovered from the sites of Lang Rongrien and Moh Khiew, Krabi Province. Carbon 14 dates of this cultural layer from both the sites range between 37,000+ 1780 B.P and 25,000 B.P. In the excavations at Sai Yok Cave in Kanchanaburi province of Western Thailand by van Heekeren and Knuth (1967), a series of unretouched micro-blades were recovered from the Mesolithic layers. Similar industries have been reported from Island Southeast Asia. Evolved blades, short blades are the terms used to define these unretouched blade flakes. The explanation given for the existence of this generalized tool kit in this part of the world is that specialised tools in this region was made of organic material like bamboo and wood. The unretouched flakes with a sharp edge was used for making these tools. They were processing tools. The bamboo tools were light in weight and could be shaped into tools by investing much less time and energy. In the Ganol-Rongram valley too a similar situation can be perceived resulting in the development of the flake-blade assemblage. As no absolute dates are available from the study area it is difficult to say if they were contemporary with the Southeast Asian assemblages mentioned above. But stratigraphically they occur within a horizon which is a late Pleistocene formation. On this basis this assemblage with the bifaces and pebble tools can be relatively dated to the late\terminal Pleistocene period-early Holocene period.

In the absence of absolute dates from the study area only hypothetical conclusions can be made. This is a major hindrance in the reconstruction of the prehistoric society of the region. The geological units within which the assemblages occur have been dated from different parts of Northeast India on the basis of which these assemblages have been relatively dated. But attempts should be made in the future to recover material for radiocarbon dating by planned excavations. As the study area is presently under occupation with the increase in population the archaeological record is liable to be disturbed. An extensive recording of the data must be undertaken before it is completely lost. In the present study

maximum amount of the data in the upper and middle course of the Ganol and Rongram river has been recorded. But due to certain peculiar local conditions, outlined in Chapter-3 recording of a negligible amount of data was not possible. The Ganol and Rongram valleys has received maximum attention from the archaeologists of the region. A few of the sites like Rongram IB site, Selbal Bichik, Missimagiri have been often reported by previous workers. This has caused significant change in the artifact density. For interpreting the density of artifacts the inventory list prepared by the previous workers has been referred for in this study. Lithic artifacts from the area housed at the District Museum, Tura, Archaeological Survey of India, Guwahati and in the museum of the Dept. of Anthropology, Gauhati University have also been studied. In spite of these limitations on the basis of the data base created, the identification of the context of the artifacts, the local environmental conditions which influenced the development of the distinctive character of the lithic assemblage peculiar to the region and the inferences drawn on the settlement and subsistence pattern of the stone-age inhabitants of the area are some of the major contributions of this thesis.

REFERENCES

Adams, W.Y. and E.W. Adams 1991. *Archaeological Typology and Practical Reality: A Dialetical Approach to Artifact Classification.* Cambridge: Cambridge University Press.

Addington, L.R. 1986, *Lithic Illustration.* Chicago: The University Press.

Agrawal, D.P. and M. Yadava 1995. *Dating the Human Past.* Pune: Indian Society for Prehistoric and Quaternary Studies.

Agrawal, D.P., R. Dodia, and M. Seth. 1990. South-Asian Climate and Environment at 18 000 BP in *The World at 18 000 BP* (O. Soffer and C. Gamble Eds.) Vol. II, pp. 231-236. London: Unwin Hyman.

Akazawa, T. and E.T.E. Szathmary 1996. *Prehistoric Mongoloid Dispersals.* Oxford: Oxford University Press.

Ali, A.A. 1998. Archaeological Remains and Further Prospects in Arunachal Pradesh, *Purattatva* 28: 64-76.

Allchin, F.R. 1957. The Neolithic Stone Industry of North Karnataka Region, *Bulletin of the School of Oriental and African Studies* XIX: 321-335.

Allen, B.C. 1980. *Gazetteer of the Khasi and Jaintia Hills, Garo Hills, Lushai Hills,* pp. 55-69. Delhi: Mittal Publications.

Allen, B.C., E.A Gait, C.G.H. Allen and H.F. Howard 1979. *Gazetteer of Bengal and Northeast India,* pp. 501-511. Delhi: Mittal Publications.

Allen, H. 1990. A Review of the Late Pleistocene/Early Recent Stone Tool Assemblages of Java, *Bulletin of the Indo-Pacific Prehistory Association,* 14th IPPA Congress, Yogyakarta (P. Bellwood Ed.), pp 37-45.

Amick, D.S. and R.P. Mauldin 1989. *Experiments in Lithic Technology.* Oxford: BAR International Series No 528.

Anderson, D.D. 1988. Excavations of a Pleistocene Rockshelter in Krabi and the Prehistory of Southern Thailand in Prehistoric Studies, in *Stone and Metal Ages in Thailand* (P. Charoenwongsa and B. Bronson Eds.), pp. 43-56. Bangkok: Thai Antiquity Group with the support of the John. F. Kennedy Foundation of Thailand.

Anderson, D.D. 1990. *Lang Rongrien Rockshelter: A Pleistocene-Early Holocene Archaeological Site from Krabi, Southwestern Thailand.* Philadelphia: University Museum Monograph 71, University of Pennsylvania.

Ascher, R. 1961. Analogy in Archaeological Explanation, *Southwestern Journal of Archaeology* 17(4): 317-325.

Bahn, P. and C. Renfrew 1991. *Archaeology, Theory, Method and Practice.* New York: Thames & Hudson.

Bailey, G.N. and P. Callow (Eds.) 1986. *Stone age Prehistory.* Cambridge: Cambridge University Press.

Balfour, H. 1917. Some types of Native Hoes: Naga Hills, *Man* XVIII(74): 105-107.

Bannanurag, R. 1988. Evidence For Ancient Woodworking: A Microwear Study of Hoabinhian Stone Tools, in *Stone and Metal Ages in Thailand* (P. Charoenwongsa and B. Bronson Eds.), pp. 61-77. Bangkok: Thai Antiquity Group with the support of the John. F. Kennedy Foundation of Thailand.

Bartstra, G.J. 1976. *Contributions to the Study of the Palaeolithic Patjitanian Culture. Java. Indonesia, Part I.* Leiden: E.J. Brill.

Basa, K. and P. Mohanty (Eds.) 2000. *Archaeology of Orissa.* New Delhi: Pratibha Prakashan.

Basak, B. 1997. *Prehistoric Settlement Patterns of the Tarafeni Valley, Midnapore District, West Bengal,* Unpublished Ph.D. Dissertation. Pune: Deccan College.

Basak, B., G.L. Badam, A. Kshirsagar and S.N. Rajguru 1998. Late Quaternary Environment Palaeontology and Culture of Tarafeni Valley, Midnapore District, West Bengal-A Preliminary Study, *Journal of Geological Society of India* 51: 731-740.

Bates, R.L. and J.A. Jackson (Eds.) 1980. *Glossary of Geology.* Virginia: American Geological Institute.

Beckerman, S. 1983. Bari Swidden Gardens: Crop Segregation Patterns, *Journal of Human Ecology* 11(1): 85.

Beckerman, S. 1983. Does the Swidden Ape the Jungle?, *Journal of Human Ecology* 11(1): 1-10.

Bellwood, P. 1978. *Man's Conquest of the Pacific.* Auckland: William Collins Publishers Ltd.

Bellwood, P. 1985. *Prehistory of the Indo-Malayan Archipelago*. Australia: Academic Press.

Bellwood, P. 1987. *Polynesians: Prehistory of an Island People*. London: Thames and Hudson.

Bettinger, R.L. 1991. *Hunter-Gatherers, Archaeological and Evolutionary Theory*. New York: Plenum Press.

Bigarella, J.J. and D. de Andrade Lima 1982. Palaeoenvironmental Changes in Brazil in *Biological Diversification in the Tropics* (G.T. Prance Ed.), pp. 27-39. New York: Columbia.

Binford, L.R. 1979. Organization and Formation Processes: Looking at Curated technologies, *Journal of Anthropological Research* 35: 255-273.

Binford, L.R. 1980. Willow Smoke and Dog's Tails: Hunter-Gatherer Settlement Systems and Archaeological Site Formation, *American Antiquity* 45: 4-20.

Binford, L.R. 1982. The Archaeology of Place, *Journal of Anthropological Archaeology* 1: 5-31.

Binford, L.R. 1988. *In Pursuit of the Past*, pp. 195-214, London: Thames and Hudson.

Binford, L.R. 1992. Seeing the Present and Interpreting the Past- and Keeping Things straight in *Space, Time and Archaeological Landscapes* (J. Rossignol and L. Wandsnider Eds.), pp. 43-59. New York and London: Plenum Press,

Bintliff, J.L. (Ed.) 1988. *Conceptual Issues in Environmental Archaeology*. Edinburg: The Edinburg University Press.

Birkeland, P.W. 1974. *Pedology, Weathering and Geomorphological Research*. London: Oxford University Press.

Birot, P. 1968. *The Cycles of Erosion in Different Climates*. London: Batsford.

Blackwood, B. 1950. *The Technology of the Modern Stone Age People in New Guinea*. Oxford: Oxford University Press.

Boriskovsky, P.I. 1966. Basic Problems of the Prehistoric Archaeology of Vietnam, *Asian Perspectives* IX: 83-85.

Botha, G.A. and T.C. Partridge 2000. Colluvial Deposits in *The Cenozoic of Southern Africa* (T.C. Partridge and R.R. Maud Eds.), pp. 88-98. Oxford: Oxford University Press.

Botha, G.A., J.M. Devillers and V. Vonbrunn 1990. Pedostratigraphy: An Analysis of Different Systems of Nomenclature and their Application to Subdivision of the Masotcheni Formation, South Africa, in *Proceedings of the IXth biennial conference of Southern African Society For Quaternary Research* at the University of Durban, 1-4th February (R.R. Maud Ed.). A.A. Balkema/Rotterdam/Brookfield.

Bradley, R.S. 1985. *Quaternary Paleoclimatology*. London: Allen and Unwin.

Brakendridge, R.G. 1980. Widespread Episodes of Stream Erosion During the Holocene and their Cause. *Nature* 283: 655-656.

Brodrible, C. 1970. *Drawings for Archaeology*. London: John Baker.

Bronson, B. and S. Natapintu 1988. Don Noi: A New Flaked Tool Industry of the Middle Holocene in Western Thailand, in *Stone and Metal Ages in Thailand* (P. Charoenwongsa and B. Bronson Eds.), pp. 91-105. Bangkok: Thai Antiquity Group with the support of the John. F. Kennedy Foundation of Thailand.

Brooks, A.S. and J.E. Yellen 1987. The Preservation of Activity Areas in the Archaeological Record: Ethnoarchaeological and Archeological Work in Northwest Ngamiland, Botswana, in *Method and Theory for Activity area Research: an ethnoarchaeological Approach* (S. Kent Ed.), pp. 63-106. New York: Columbia University Press

Brooks, R.L. 1993. Household Abandonment Among Sedentary Plain Societies: Behavioural Sequences and Consequences, in Interpretation of the Archaeological Record in *Abandonment of Settlements and Regions* (C.M. Cameroon and S.A. Tomka Eds.), pp. 178-90. Cambridge: Cambridge University Press.

Butzer, K.W. 1971. *Environment and Archaeology*. Chicago: Aldine.

Butzer, K.W. 1987. *Archaeology as Human Ecology*. Cambridge: Cambridge University Press.

Cameron, C.M. and S.A. Tomka 1993. *Abandonment of Settlement and Regions*: Cambridge University Press.

Chang, K.C. 1970. The Beginnings of Agriculture in the Far East, *Antiquity* 44: 175-85.

Chang, K.C. 1972. Settlements Patterns in Archaeology, in *Module in Anthropology*, pp. 1-26. Phillipines: Addison-Wesley Publication.

Charlton, T.H. 1981. Archaeology, Etnohistory and Ethnology: Interpretive interfaces in Advances in Archeological Method and Theory (M.B. Schiffer Ed.), pp. 129-176. Academic Press: New York

Charoenwangsa, P. and B. Bronson 1988. Introduction: Prehistoric Chronology in Thailand, in *Prehistoric Studies: The Stone and Metal Ages in Thailand* (P. Charoenwangsa and B. Bronson Eds.), pp. 1-14. Bangkok: Thai Antiquity Working Group.

Chatterji, S.K. 1974. *Kirata-Jana-Krti*. Calcutta: The Asiatic Society.

Chen, Te-K'un 1959. *Archaeology in China*, Vol-I. Cambridge: Heffer & San Ltd.

Cherry, J.F., J.L. Davis and E. Montzourani 1991. *Landscape Archaeology as Long Term History*. California: UCLA Institute of Archaeology.

Childe, V.G. 1936. *Man Makes Himself*. London: Watts.

Childe, V.G. 1951. *Social Evolution*. New York: Henry Schuman.

Choudhury, B.N. 1969. *Cultural and Linguistic Aspects of Garos*. Gauhati: Lawyers Book Stall.

Choudhury, J.N. 1991. Prehistoric and Early Migration in Northeast India in *Archaeology of North-Eastern India* (G. Sengupta and J.P. Singh Eds.), pp. 86-105. Shillong: Northeast Hill University.

Chung, T.N. 1994. The Son Vi Culture: Technology and Typology. Paper Presented in the 15th *Indo Pacific Prehistoric Association Congress* (IPPA): Chiang Mai, Thailand.

Cohen, D. and J. Mayerson 1977. Subsurface Movements of Stone Artifacts and their Implications for the Prehistory of Central Africa, *Nature* 266: 812-815.

Colani, M. 1927. *L'age de la pierre dans la province de Hoabinh (Tonkin)*. Hanoi: Memoirs de la Service Geologique d'Indichine.

Coles, J.M. and E.S. Higgs 1969. *The Archaeology of Early Man*. London: Faber and Faber.

Corvinus, G. 1994. The Prehistory of Nepal after 10 years of Research. Paper presented in the 15th IPPA Congress: Chiang Mai, Thailand.

Cotterel, B. and J. Kamminga 1987. The Formation of Flakes, *American Antiquity* 52: 675-708.

Cullen, J.L. 1981. Microfossil Evidence for Changing Salinity Patterns in the Bay of Bengal Over the last 20,000 years, *Palaeogeography, Palaeoclimatology, Palaeoecology* 35: 315-356. Amsterdam: Elsvier Scientific Publishing Company.

Dani, A.H. 1960. *Prehistory and Protohistory of Eastern India*. Calcutta: Firma K.L. Mukhopadhyay.

Datta, A. 1992. *Neolithic Culture in West Bengal*. Delhi: Agam Kala Prakashan.

De Terra, H., and T.T. Paterson 1936. Observations on the Upper Siwalik Formations and Later Prehistoric Deposits in India. *Proceedings of the Prehistoric Society* 76: 791-822.

Debenath, A. and H.L. Dibble 1994. *Handbook of Palaeolithic Typology*. Pennsylvania: University Museum.

Dewar, R.E. and K.V. McBride 1992. Remnant Settlement Patterns in *Space, Time and Archaeological Landscapes* (J. Rossignol and L. Wandsnider Eds.), pp. 227-252. New York: Plenum Press.

Dheeradilok, P. 1992. Quaternary Geological Formations of Thailand: Their Depositional Environments, Economic Significance and Tectonics, in *Proceedings of the National Conference on "Geologic Resources of Thailand: Potential for Future Development"* 17th-24th November, pp. 600-607. Bangkok: Dept. of Mineral Resources.

Dheeradilok, T. Wongwanich, W. Tansathien and P. Chaodumrong 1992. An Introduction to Geology of Thailand, in *Proceedings of the National Conference on "Geologic Resources of Thailand: Potential for Future Development"* 17th-24th November, pp. 737-741. Bangkok: Dept. of Mineral Resources.

Dibble, H.L. and Bar-Yosef 1995. *Definition and Interpretation of Levallois Technology*. Madison: Prehistory Press.

Drucker, P. 1972. Stratigraphy in Archaeology: an Introduction in *Module in Anthropology*, pp. 30-1 to 30-16. Phillipines: Addison-Wesley Publication.

Dunnel, R.C. and W. Dancey 1983. The Siteless Survey: A Regional Scale Data Collection Strategy, in *Advances Archaeological Method and Theory* 6 (M.B.

Schiffer Ed.), pp. 267-287. New York: Academic Press.

Duplessy, J.C. 1982. Glacial to Interglacial Contrasts in the Northern Indian Ocean, *Nature* 295: 494-498.

Dwyer, P.D. 1985. Choice and Constraint in a Papua New Guinea Food Quest, *Journal of Human Ecology* 13(1): 49.

Eden, M. J. 1993. Swidden Cultivation in Forest and Savanna in Lowland Southwest Papua New Guninea, *Journal of Human Ecology* 21(2): 145.

Eden, M.J. and A. Andrade 1987. Ecological aspects of Swidden Cultivation among the Andoke and Witoto Indians of the Colombian Amazon Zambia. *Journal of Human Ecology* 15(3): 339.

Fisher, C.A. 1964. *Southeast Asia: Social, Economic and Political Geography.* London.

Flowers, N.M., D.R. Gross, M.L. Ritter and D.W. Werner 1982. Variation in Swidden Practices in Four Central Brazilian Indian Societies, *Journal of Human Ecology* 10(2): 203.

Foley, R. 1981. A Model of Regional Archaeological Structure, *Proceedings of Pre-Historic Society* 47: 1-17.

Foley, R. 1981. Off-Site Archaeology: An Alternative Approach for the Short-Sited in *Patterns of the Past: Studies in Honour of David Clark* (I. Hodder, G. Issac and N. Hammond Eds.), pp. 157-183. Cambridge: Cambridge University Press.

Fox, R. 1970. *The Tabon Caves: Archaeological Exploration and Excavations on Palawan Island, Phillipines.* Manila: Manila National Museum Monograph No.1.

Frink, D.S. 1984: Artifact Behaviour Within the Plow Zone, *Journal of Field Archaeology* 11:356-363.

Geological Survey of India-Miscellaneous Publication 30: Geology and Mineral Resources of India, Part IV-Arunachal Pradesh, Assam, Manipur, Meghalaya, Mizoram, Nagaland and Tripura. *Calcutta: Government of India.*

Ghosh, A.K. 1974. Stratigraphy and Typology of Flake-Blade Industries in Eastern India, Paper presented in the Seminar on Indian Prehistory and Protohistory, June 25-29, 1974. Poona: Deccan College.

Ghosh, A.K. 1977. What Happens when Cultural and Biological Ability of Man Fails? A Case Study with the Palaeolithic Period in the Garo Hills. Cultural and Biological Adaptability of Man with Special Reference to Northeast India . *Bulletin of the Dept. of Anthropology.* Dibrugarh: Dibrugarh University.

Ghosh, A.K. 1979. Prehistoric Cultures of North Eastern India: Rethinking of the Problem and the Methodology, Paper Presented in the Conference on History and Culture of North-East India, North-Eastern Hill University (NEHU), Shillong.

Ghosh, A.K. 1984. Faunal Resources of Garo Hills: Need for Conservation in *Garo Hills Land and People* (L.S. Gassah Ed.), pp. 72-104. New Delhi: Omsons Publications.

Gifford, D.P. 1978. Ethnoarchaeological Observations of Natural Processes Affecting Cultural Materials, in *Exploration in Ethnoarchaeology* (R.A. Gould Ed.), pp. 77-101. Albuquerque: University of New Mexico Press.

Glover, I.C. 1973. Late Stone Age Traditions in Southeast Asia, in *South Asian Archaeology* (N. Hammond Ed.), pp. 51-65. London: Duckworth.

Glover, I.C. 1977. The Hoabinhian Hunter-Gatherers or Early Agriculturists in Southeast Asia in *Hunters, Gatherers and First Farmers Beyond Europe* (J.V.S. Megaw Ed.), pp. 145-166. Leiceister: Leceister University Press.

Godwin Austen, H.H. 1875. A Celt Found in the Khasi Hills at Shillong. *Proceedings of the Asiatic Society of Bengal*: 158-59.

Goldberg, P., D.T. Nash, and M.D. Petragalia 1993. *Formation Processes in Archaeological Context.* Monographs in World Archaeology No. 17. Madison: Prehistory Press.

Gorman, C. 1969. Hoabinhian: A Pebble Tool Complex with Early Plant Association in Southeast Asia, *Science* 163: 671-673.

Gorman, C.F. 1970. Excavations at Spirit Cave, North Thailand: Some Interim Interpretations, *Asian Perspectives* XII: 79-107.

Gorman, C.F. 1970. The Hoabinhian and After: Subsistence Patterns in Southeast Asia During the Late Pleistocene and Early Recent Periods, *World Archaeology* 2: 300-320.

Goswami, D.N.D. 1950. *Geology of Assam*. Guwahati: Gauhati University.

Goswami, D.N.D. 1968. Environmental Significance During the Palaeocene-Lower Eocene Period in the Western Part of Meghalaya (Garo Hills), in Proceedings of the Pre-Congress Symposium and Field Study Meeting on the Physical Geography of Western Himalaya and the Meghalaya Plateau, 21st International Geographical Congress, India. Guwahati: Gauhati University.

Goswami, M.C. and A.C. Bhagwati 1959a. A Typological Study of Shouldered Celt from Renchengiri (Garo Hills), *Journal of the University of Gauhati* X(2): 105-22.

Goswami, M.C. and A.C. Bhagwati 1959b. A Preliminary Report on a Collection of Neolithic Tool Types from Western Assam, *Man in India* XXXIX(4): 312-24.

Gould, R.A. 1961. *Living Archaeology*. New York: Cambridge University Press.

Gupta, A. 1988: Large Floods as Geomorphic Events in the Humid Tropics, in *Flood Geomorphology* (V.R. Baker, R.C. Kochel and P.C. Patton Eds.), pp. 301-315. New York: Wiley.

Hames, R. 1983. Monoculture, Polyculture, and Polyvariety in Tropical Forest Swidden Cultivation, *Journal of Human Ecology* 11(1): 13.

Hammersley, M. and P. Alheinson 1983. *Ethnography*. London: Tavistock Publishers.

Haridasan, K. and R.R. Rao 1984. Flora, Vegetation and Plant Resources of Garo Hills in *Garo Hills Land and People* (L.S. Gassah Ed.), pp. 97-104. New Delhi: Omsons Publications.

Harlan, J. 1975. *Crops and Man*. Madison: American Society of Agronomy.

Harlan, J. 1976. *Origin of African Plant Domestication*. Paris: Mouton Publishers.

Harrison, T. 1957. The Great Cave of Niah; A Preliminary Report on Bornean Prehistory, *Man 57:* 161-165.

Hassan, F.A. 1985. Palaeoenvironments and Contemporary Archaeology: A Geoarchaeological Approach, in *Archaeological Geology* (G. Rapp Jr. and A. Gifford Eds.), pp. 87-99. London: Yale University Press.

Hasternath, S. 1991. *Climate Dynamics of the Tropics*. Kluwer: Academic Publishers.

Hayden, B. 1989. From Chopper to Celt: the Evolution of Resharpening Techniques in *Time, Energy and Stone Tools* (R. Torrence Ed.), pp. 7-16. Cambridge: Cambridge University Press.

Heekeren, van. H.R. and Count Eigil Knuth 1967. *Archaeological Excavations in Thailand* Vol. I. Copenhagen: Munksgaard.

Henry, D.O. 1989. *From Foraging to Agriculture*. Pennsylvania: University of Pennsylvania Press.

Higham, C.F.W. 1989a. *The Archaeology of Mainland Southeast Asia*. Cambridge: Cambridge University Press.

Higham, C.F.W. 1989b. The Later Prehistory of Mainland Southeast Asia, *Journal of World Prehistory* 3(3): 235-279.

Higham, C.F.W. 1990. *The Excavation of Khok Phanom Di*. London: The Societies of Antiquaries of London.

Higham, C.F.W. and R.H. Parker 1970. *Prehistoric Research in Northeast Thailand, 1969-1970: A Preliminary Report*. Dunedin: Department of Anthropology, University of Otago.

Holliday, T.V. 1992. *Soils in Archaeology*. Washington: Smithsonian Institution Press.

Hutterer, K.L. 1976. An Evolutionary Approach to the Southeast Asian Cultural Sequence, *Current Anthropology* 17(2): 221-240.

Hutton, J.H. 1965. The Mixed Culture of the Naga Tribes, *Journal of the Royal Anthropological Institute* 95(1): 16-43.

IAR Indian Archaeological Review 1963-64 to 1979-80.

Inizan, M., Helene-Roche, J. Tixier and M. Reduron 1992. *Technology of Kna*pped *Stone*. MEUDON Cedex, France: Centre de Recherches Archeologiques.

Isaac, G.L. and J.W.K. Harris 1975. Scatter between Patches. Paper presented to the Kroeber Anthropological Society.

Jochim, M.A. 1991. Archaeology as Long Term Ethnography, *American Anthropologist* 93(2): 308-321.

Johnson, A.M and J.R. Rodine 1984. Debris Flows, in *Slope Instability* (Brunsden D. and D.B. Prior Eds.), pp. 257-355. New York: John Wiley and Sons.

Kelly, R.L. 1988. The Three Sides of Biface, *American Antiquity* 53(4): 714-34.

Kennedy, K.A.R. 1993 Evolution of South Asian Pleistocene Hominids: Demic Displacement or Regional Continuity in *South-Asian Archaeology* 1 (A. Parpaola and P. Koshikallio Eds.), pp. 337-343.

84

Kent, S. 1952. *Analyzing Activity Areas.* Albuquerque: University of New Mexico Press.

Kramer, C. (Ed.) 1979. *Ethnoarchaeology: Implications of Ethnography for Archaeology.* New York: Columbia University Press.

Krishan, M.S. 1960. *Geology of India and Burma.* Madras: Higginbothams Pvt.Ltd.

Kwang-Chi, Chang 1970. Prehistoric Archaeology of Taiwan, *Asian Perspectives* XIII: 59-77.

Lamburg-Karlovsky, C.C. 1979: *Hunters, Farmers and Civilizations: Old World Archaeology.* San Francisco, W.H. Freeman & Co.

Lehmul, F. J. Bohner & Frank Haselein. 1999. Late Quarternary Environmental Changes and Human Occupation of the Tibetan Plateau, *Man and Environment* XXIV(1): 137-144.

Logan, A.C. 1960. *Old Chipped stones in India.* Calcutta: Thacker Spink & Co.

Mahanta, H.C. 1995. *A Study on the Stone Age Cultures of Selbalgiri, West Garo Hills, Meghalaya.* Unpublished Ph.D. Dissertation. Guwahati: Gauhati University.

Majumdar, D.N. 1956. *Garos.* Gauhati: Lawyers Book Stall.

Majumdar, D.N. 1978. *Culture Change in Two Garo Villages.* Calcutta: Anthropological Survey of India.

Manner, H.I. 1981. Ecological Succession in New and Old Swiddens of Montane Papua New Guinea, *Journal of Human Ecology* 9(3): 359.

Maringer, J. 1957. Some Tools of Early Hoabinhian Type from Central Japan, *Man* 57(1): 1-3.

Mathews, J.M. 1966. A Review of the 'Hoabinhian' in Indo-China, *Asian Perspectives* IX: 86-95.

Mathews, J.M. 1966. The Hoabinhian Affinities of Some Australian Assemblages, *Archaeology and Physical Anthropology in Oceania* 1: 5-22.

McCarthy, F.D. 1940. Comparison of the Prehistory of Australia with that of Indo-China, the Malay Peninsula and the Netherlands East Indies, *Proceedings of the Third Congress of Prehistorians of the Far East,* pp. 30-50.

McCarthy, F.D. 1941. Two Pebble Industry Sites of Hoabinhian 1 type on the north coast of New South Wales, *Records of the Australian Museum* 21: 21-27.

Mcgrath, D.G. 1987. The Role of Biomass in Shifting Cultivation, *Journal of Human Ecology* 15(2): 221.

Medhi, D.K. 1974. A Study on the Stratigraphy of the River Rongram in the Garo Hills in *Contemporary Anthropological Research in Northeast India* (B.M. Das Ed.), pp. 143-146. Dibrugarh: Dibrugarh University.

Medhi, D.K. 1977. Some Aspects of Quarternary Studies in the Garo Hills, Meghalaya, *Bulletin of the Deccan College Post Graduate &Research Institute* 37(1): 71-78.

Medhi, D.K. 1980. *Quarternary History of the Garo Hills, Meghalay.* Unpublished Ph.D. Dissertation. Pune: Deccan College.

Megaw, J.V.S. (Ed.) 1980. *Hunters,Gatherers and First Farmers Beyond Europe: An Archaeological Survey.* Leiceister: The University Press.

Memoirs of the Indian Meterological Department XXXI(III): Monthly and Annual Normals of Rainfall and of Rainy Days: Based on Records from 1901-1950, pp. 71.

Mishra, S., S.B. Ota, G. Shete, S. Naik and B.C. Deotare 1999. Late Quarternary Alluvial History and Archaeological Sites in the Nimar Region of Western Madhya Pradesh, India, *Man and Environment* XXIV(1): 149-155.

Mishra, S., S.N. Rajguru, Sonali Naik, S. Ghate and A. Kshirsagar 1998. Climatic Change during the Pleistocene/Holocene Transition in Upland Western Maharashtra, Western India in *Water, Environment and Society in Times of Climatic Change* (A.S. Issar and N. Brown Eds.), pp. 323-333. Netherlands: Kluwer Academic Publishers.

Misra, V.N. 1978. The Acheulian Industry of Rock Shelter IIIF-23 at Bhimbetka, Central India, *Australian Archaeology* 8: 63-106.

Movius, Hallam L. Jr. 1948. The Lower Palaeolithic Cultures of Southern and Eastern Asia. *Transactions of the American Philosophical Society* Vol. XXXVIII: 329-420.

Murray, T. and A.J. Walker 1988. Like WHAT? A Practical Question of Analogical Inference and Archaeological Meaning, *Journal of Anthropological Archaeology* 7(1): 248-288.

Murty, M.L.K. 1979. Recent Research on the Upper Palaeolithic Phase in India, *Journal of Field Archaeology* 6(3): 301-320.

Narayan, B. 1996. *Prehistoric Archaeology of Bihar*. Patna: K.P. Jayaswal Research Institute.

Narayan, B. 1999. *Emerging Issues of Prehistory in Bihar*. Calcutta: Centre for Archaeological Studies & Training, Eastern India.

Nash, D.T. and M.D. Petraglia 1987. *Natural Formation Processes and the Archaeological Record*. Oxford: BAR International Series No 352.

Nelson, M. 1991. The Study of Technological Organization in *Archaeological Method and Theory* (M.B. Schiffer Ed.) 3: 57-100.

Nishimura, M. 1996. Implication from Regional Variability and Termination of the Hoabinhian industry: A Perspective from Revising the Present Data, Paper presented in the 14th Congress of the Indo-Pacific Prehistory Association: Chiangmai, Thailand.

Orme, B. 1973. Archaeology and Ethnography in *Explanation of Cultural Change* (C. Renfrew Ed.), pp. 481-92. London: Duckworth.

Overpeck, J, D. Anderson, S. Trumbore and W. Prell 1996. The Southwest Indian Monsoon over the last 18,000 years, *Climate Dynamics* 12: 213-225.

Paddayya, K. 1984. *India: Old Stone Age*. Neve Forschungen Zur altsteinzeit Sonderdruck.

Paddayya, K. 1995a. Investigation of Man-Environment relationships in Indian Archaeology: Some Theoretical Considerations, *Man and Environment* XIX (1-2): 1-28.

Paddayya, K. 1995b. Theoretical Perspective in Indian Archaeology: an historical review in *Theory in Archaeology, A World Perspective* (P.J. Ucko Ed.), pp.110-144. London: Routledge.

Pakem, B., J.B. Bhattacharys, B.B. Dutta and B. Datta Ray (Eds.) 1976. *Shifting Cultivation in Northeast India*. Shillong: Northeast Council of Social Science Research.

Pant, P.C. and V. Jayaswal 1977-78. Jamalpur: A Typological Variant Within the Middle Palaeolithic Culture- Complex of India, *Purattatva* 9: 15-34.

Pascoe, E.H. 1963. *A Manual of the Geology of India and Burma* (3rd Ed.). Geological Survey, Govt. of India.

Peer, P.V. 1992. *Levallois Reduction Strategy*. Monographs in World Archaeology No. 13. Wisconsin: Madison.

Pei, Wen-Chung 1931. Notice on the discovery of quartz and other stone artifacts in the Lower Pleistocene Hominid-Bearing Sediments of the Choukoutien Cave deposits. *Bulletin of the Geological Society of China* 11: 109-139.

Penny, Dan 1999. Pollen Grains in Sands of Time Lake Sediments Contribute to the Archaeology of Thailand, *Expedition* 41(3): 32-36. Pennsylvania: The Magazine of the University of Pennsylvania Museum of Archaeology and Anthropology.

Piper, C.S. 1966. *Soil and Plant analysis*. Bombay: Hans Publishers.

Plog, S.F. and W. Wait 1978. Decision Making in Modern Surveys in *Advances in Archaeological Method and Theory* 1(M.B. Schiffer Ed.), pp. 383-421. New York: Academic Press.

Pookajorn, S. 1984. *The Technological and Functional Morphological Analysis of the Lithic Tools From the Hoabinhian Excavation At the Ban Kao Area; Kanchanaburi Province, Thailand*. Bangkok: Faculty of Archaeology, Silpakorn University, Bangkok 10200, Thailand.

Pookajorn, S. and Staff 1991. *Preliminary excavations at Moh-Khiew Cave, Krabi Province, Sakai Cave, Trang Province and Ethnoarchaeological Research of Hunter-Gatherer Group, so called 'Sakai' or 'Semang' at Trang Province*, Vol. I. Bangkok: The Hoabinhian Research Project in Thailand.

Pope, G. 1989. Bamboo and Human Evolution, *Natural History* 57(10): 49-57.

Pope, G.G., S. Barr, A. Macdonald and S. Nakabalang 1986. Earliest Radiometrically Dated Artifacts from Southeast Asia, *Current Anthropology* 27(3): 275-280.

Prakash, P.V. 1994. Excavations at Paradesipalem: A Neolithic Cultural Complex, *Man and Environment* XIX(2): 267-274.

Prakash, V. 1998. Vengasarai: A Mesolithic Cave in the Eastern Ghats, Andhra Pradesh, *Man and Environment* XXIII(2): 1-16.

Prance, G.T. 1982 *Biological Diversification in the Tropics*. Columbia: Columbia University Press.

Pratap, A. 2000. *The Hoe and the Axe- An Ethnohistory of Shifting Cultivation in Eastern India*. New Delhi: Oxford University Press.

Prishanchit, S. 1998. A Preliminary Survey of Lithic Industries in Mae Hong Son, Nan and Uttaradit, Northern Thailand in *The Stone and Metal Ages in Thailand* (P. Charoenwongsa and B. Bronson Eds.), pp. 81-89. Bangkok: Thai Antiquity Group with the support of the John.F.Kennedy Foundation of Thailand.

Quaritch, Wales H.G. 1967. *Indianization of China & Southeast Asia*. London: Bernard Quaritch Ltd.

Raiz, E. 1962. *Principles of Cartography*. New York: McGraw Hill Book Company, Inc.

Rajguru, S.N. 1978. On the problem of Acheulian Chronology in Western and Southern India. Paper presented in the Post Plenary Symposium on 'Recent Advances in Indo-Pacific Prehistory, December 19-22, 1978. Deccan College, Pune-6.

Rajguru, S.N. 1983. Problem of Late Pleistocene Aridity in India. *Man and Environment* VI: 107-111.

Rajguru, S.N. and S. Mishra 1997. Late Quaternary climatic change in India: A Geoarchaeological Approach. *Bulletin of the Indo-Pacific Prehistory Association* 16 (P. Bellwood and D. Tillotson Eds.), pp. 27-31. Canberra: Australian National University.

Ramesh, N.R. 1986. Discovery of Stone Age tools from Tripura and its Relevance to Prehistory of Southeast Asia, *GEOSEA Proceedings, Geological Society Malaysia Bulletin*, Vol. II, pp.289-310.

Ramesh, N.R. and G. Rajagopalan 1999. Late Quarternary Sediments of North-Eastern India: A Review. *Gondwana Geological Magazine* Vol. 14(1): 13-35.

Rao, N. 1994. Subsistence and Associated Settlement Patterns in Central India: An Ethnoarchaeological Analysis in *Living Traditions* (B. Allchin Ed.), New Delhi: Oxford & IBH Publishing Co. Pvt. Ltd.

Rao, S.N. 1976. Continuity and Survival of Neolithic traditions in Northeastern India, *Asian Perspectives* XX(2): 191-204.

Rao, S.N. 1977. Excavation at Sarutaru; A Neolithic Site in Assam, *Man and Environment* I: 39-43.

Rapp, R. and J.A. Gifford (Eds.) 1985. *Archaeological Geology*. New Haven: Yale University Press.

Ray, R. 1986. *Ancient Settlement Patterns of Eastern India*. Calcutta: Pearl Publications.

Redman, C.L. and P.J. Watson 1970. Systematic and Intensive Surface Collection, *American Antiquity* 35: 279-291.

Renfrew, C. and P. Bahn 1993. *Archaeology*. London: Thames and Hudson.

Reynolds, T.E.G. 1990. Problems of the Stone Age of Thailand, *The Journal of the Siam Society* 78(1): 109-113.

Ronquillo, Wilfredo P. 1981. *The Technological and Functional analysis of the lithic flake tools from Rabel Cave, northern Luzon, Phillipines*. Manila: National Museum of the Phillipines

Rosen, S.A. 1997. *LITHICS After the Stone Age*. London: Alta Mira Press. A Division of Sage Publications Inc.

Rouse, I. 1986. *Migrations in Prehistory*. Yale: Yale University.

Roy, S.K. 1981. Aspects of Neolithic Agriculture and Shifting Cultivation, Garo Hills, Meghalaya, *Asian Perspectives* XXIV(2): 193-219.

Sadakata, N., H. Maemoku, S.N. Rajguru, S. Mishra and K. Fijiwara 1995. Late Quaternary Environmental Change in the Pravara River Basin, Northwestern Deccan Upland, India in *Proceedings of the International Symposium on Palaeoenvironmental Change in Tropical-Subtropical Monsoon Asia*, Special Publication no. 24, pp. 43-54. Hiroshima University: Research Center for Regional Geography.

Sangma, M.S. 1991. Crafts and Technology of the Garos in *Archaeology of North-Eastern India* (G. Sengupta and Jai Prakash Singh Eds.), pp. 304-312. Shillong: North East Hill University Publication.

Sankalia, H.D. 1964. *Stone Age Tools: Their Techniques, Names and Probable Functions*. Pune: Deccan College.

Sankalia, H.D. 1974. *The Prehistory and Protohistory of India and Pakistan*, pp. 283-98. Pune: Deccan College.

Sankalia, H.D. 1981. From History to Prehistory in Assam in *Cultural Contours of India* (Dr. Satya Prakash Felicitation

Volume Pt. II, V.S. Srivastava Ed.), pp. 1-5. Delhi: Abhinav Publications.

Sant, U. 1991. *Neolithic Settlement pattern of Northern India*. Delhi: Sarita Book House.

Santoni, M. 1992. Surveys in Northern Thailand in *Southeast Asian Archaeology 1990-Proce*edings *of the Third Conference of the European Association of Southeast Asian Archaeologists* (I. Glover Ed.), pp. 233-245. University of Hull: Centre for South-East Asian Studies,

Sauer, C.O. 1969. *Agricultural Origins*. Cambridge: M.I.T. Press.

Schepartz, L.A., S. Miller-Antonio and D.A. Bakkem 2000. Upland resources and the Early Palaeolithic Occupation of Southern China, Vietnam, Laos, Thailand and Burma in *Archaeology in Southeast Asia, World Archaeology* 32(1): 1-10.

Schiffer, M.B. 1972. Archaeological Context and Systemic Context, *American Antiquity* 37: 156-165.

Schiffer, M.B. 1983. Towards the Identification of Formation Processes, *American Antiquity* 48(4): 675-706.

Schiffer, M.B. 1987. *Formation Processes of the Archaeological Record*. Alburquerque. University of New Mexico Press.

Sellet, F. 1993. Chaine Operatoire: The Concept and its Applications. *Lithic Technology* 18(1&2): 106-111.

Sharer, R.J. and W. Ashmore 1979. *Fundamentals of Archaeology*: California: The Benjamin/ Cummings Publishing Company, Inc.

Sharma, A.K. 1996. *Early Man in Eastern Himalayas*. New Delhi: Aryan International Books,

Sharma, H.C. 1972. Stone Age cultures of the Garo Hills. Unpublished Ph.D. Dissertation: Gauhati University.

Sharma, C. and M.S. Chauhan 1994 vegetation and Climate since Last Glacial Maximum in Darjeeling (Mirik Lake), Eastern Himalayas in *Proceedings of the 29th International Geological Congress* (T. Nishiyama ed.). Brill Academic Publishers.

Sharma, T.C. 1974. Prehistory of Assam in *Indian Anthropology Today* (D. Sen Ed.), pp. 63-70. Calcutta: The Dept. of Anthropology, Calcutta University.

Sharma, T.C. 1966a. *Prehistoric Archaeology of Assam-A Study of Neolithic Cultures*. Unpublished Ph.D. Dissertation: University of London.

Sharma, T.C. 1966b. Researches on the Prehistoric Archaeology of Assam, *Journal of the Assam Science Society* IX: 1-10.

Sharma, T.C. 1967. A note on the Neolithic Pottery of Assam, *Man* 2(1): 126-128.

Sharma, T.C. 1970. The Stone Industries of Selbalgiri. *Proce*edings *of the Indian Science Congress* III (abstract).

Sharma, T.C. 1978. A Note on Some Prehistoric Survivals in North East India, *The Bulletin of the Department of Anthropology,* Dibrugarh University 7-8: 1-6.

Sharma, T.C. 1978. A Note on the Microlithic Industry of Garo Hills *in Senarat Paravitana Commemoration Volume* (L. Prematilleke, K. Indrapala and De Leeuw J.E. Van L Eds.), pp. 215-217. Leiden: E.J. Brill.

Sharma, T.C. 1979. Sources of the Pre-history of Meghalaya in *Sources of the History of India* (S.P. Sen Ed.) II, pp. 157-166. Calcutta: Institute of Historical Studies.

Sharma, T.C. 1980. Prehistoric Archaeology in North-East India- A Review of Progress in *Eastern Himalaya* (D.N. Majumdar and T.C. Sharma Eds.), pp. 102-135. Delhi: Cosmo Publication,

Sharma, T.C. 1981. The Neolithic Pattern of Northeast-India in *Madhu; Recent Researches in Indian Archaeology and Art History* (M.N. Deshpande Ed.), pp. 41-50.

Sharma, T.C. 1988. Discovery of Hoabinhian Cultural Relics in Northeast India in *Adaptation and Other Essays* (N.C. Ghosh and S. Chakraborty Eds.), pp. 136-139. Santiniketan: Visva Bharati.

Sharma, T.C. 1991. Prehistoric Situation of Northeast India in *Archaeology of North-East India* (G. Sengupta and J.P. Singh Eds.), pp. 41-56. Shillong: North East Hill University.

Sharma, T.C. and H.C. Sharma 1971. On the Discovery of Stone Age Sites in Central Garo Hills . *Journal of the Assam Science Society* XIV(1): 18-24.

Shoocongdej, R. 1990. Recent Research on the Post-Pleistocene in the Lower Khwai Noi Basin, Kanchanaburi, Western Thailand, *Bulletin of the Indo-Pacific Prehistoric Association* 1: 143-147.

Shoocongdej, R. 1996a. Rethinking the Development of Sedentary Villages in

Western Thailand. *Indo-Pacific Prehistory Association Bulletin* 14 (Chiang Mai Papers, Vol. I): 203-209.

Shoocongdej, R. 1996b. Working Toward an Anthropological Perspective on Thai Prehistory: Current Research on the Post-Pleistocene. *Indo-Pacific Prehistory Association Bulletin* 14 (Chiang Mai Papers, Vol. I): 119-128.

Shoocongdej, R. 2000. Forager Mobility Organization in Seasonal Tropical Environments of Western Thailand. *Archaeology in Southeast Asia, World Archaeology* 32(1): 14-40.

Shott, M. 1994. Size and Form in the Analysis of Flake Debris: Review and Recent Approaches, *Journal of Archaeological Method and Theory* 1(1): 69-110.

Singh, A.T. 1987. *Quaternary Studies in the Manipur Valley.* Unpublished Ph.D. Dissertation. Pune: Deccan College.

Singh, G., R. D. Joshi, S.K. Chopra & A.B. Singh 1974. Late Quarternary History of Vegetation and Climate in the Rajasthan Desert, India, *Philosophical Transactions of the Royal Society of London* 267: 467-501.

Singh, O.K. 1993. *Stone Age Cultures of Manipur,* Unpublished Ph.D. Dissertation, University of Manipur.

Singh, O.K. and T.C. Sharma 1968. Studies on Prehistoric Archaeology of the Garo-Hills (Assam), *Journal of the Assam Science Society* XI: 36-50.

Singh, R.P. 1968. Geomorphology of the Shillong Plateau of Assam in *Proceedings of the Pre-Congress Symposium and Field Study Meeting on the Physical Geography of Western Himalaya and the Meghalaya Plateau, 21st International Geographical Congress, India:* Gauhati University.

Sinha, K.K, R.K. Sinha and N.P. Varma 1983. *Progress Report for Field Season 1981-82* (unpublished), pp. 39, 47. Shillong: Geological Survey of India.

Sirocko, F., M. Sarnthein, H. Erlenkeuserg, H. Lange, M. Arnold and J.C. Duplessy 1993. Century Sale Events in Monsoonal Climate Over the Past 24,000 years, *Nature* 364: 322-324.

Small, R.J. 1987. *The study of Landforms.* Cambridge: Cambridge University Press.

Solheim, W.G.(II) 1962a. Reworking Southeast Asian Prehistory. '*Paideuma*', pp.

126-137: Mitteilungen Zur Kulturkunde Band XV.

Solheim, W.G.(II) 1964. Thailand and Prehistory, *Silpakorn Journal* 8: 42-77.

Solheim, W.G.(II) 1966. Prehistoric Archeology in Thailand, *Antiquity* 40: 8-16.

Solheim, W.G.(II) 1969. New Directions in Southeast Asian Prehistory, *Anthropologica* XI(1): 31-40.

Solheim, W.G.(II) 1970. Northern Thailand, *Asian Perspectives* XIII: 149-153.

Solheim, W.G.(II) 1962b. Southeast Asia, *Asian Perspectives* VI: 21-23.

Sonowal, M. and T.C. Sharma 1988. Studies on the Blunted Back Flake-Knives Industries of the Garo Hills, Meghalaya in *Adaptation and Other Essays* (N.C. Ghosh and S. Chakraborty Eds.), pp. 131-135. Santiniketan: Visva Bharati.

Spate, O.H.K. 1954. *India and Pakistan: A General and Regional Geography,* pp. 600. London. .

Stafford, R.C. and H.R. Edwin 1992. Landscape scale, Geoenvironmental Approaches to Prehistoric Settlement Strategies in *Space, Time and Archaeological Landscape* (J. Rossignal and L. Wandsnider Eds.), pp. 137-161. New York and London: Plenum Press.

Stocks, A. 1983. Candeshi and Cocamilla Swiddens in Eastern Peru, *Journal of Human Ecology* 11(1)-69.

Stromgaard, P. 1989. Adaptive Strategies in the Breakdown of Shifting Cultivation: The case of Mambwe, Lamba, and Lala of Northern Zambia, *Journal of Human Ecology* 17(4): 427.

Tan, Ha Van 1994. The Hoabinhian and Before. *Indo-Pacific Prehistory Association Bulletin* 16: 35-40.

Teilhard, de Chardin, Pierre and Pei Wen Chung 1932. The lithic industry of the Sinanthropus deposits in Choukoutien, *Bulletin of the Geological Society of China* 11(4): 315-364.

Thapar, B.K. 1983. *Recent Archaeological Discoveries in India,* pp. 43-44. The Centre for East Asian Cultural Studies. UNESCO.

Thomas, J. 1991. An Archaeology of difference in *Rethinking the Neolithic,* pp. 1-19. Cambridge: Cambridge University Press.

Thomas, M.F. 1994. *Geomorphology in the Tropics-A Study of Weathering and Denudation in Low Latitudes.* England: John Willey & Sons Ltd.

Thompson, R.H. 1956. The subjective element in Archaeological Inference, *Southwestern Journal of Anthropology* 12: 327-332.

Tilley, C. 1996: *An Ethnography on the Neolithic*. Cambridge: University press.

Tiwari, S.K. 1985. *Zoo geography of India and Southeast Asia*. Delhi: CBS Publisher.

Tomka, S.A. and M.G. Stevenson 1993. Understanding abandonment processes: Summary and remaining concerns in *Abandonment of Settlement and Regions: ethnoarchaeological and archaeological approaches* (C.A. Cameron and S.A. Tomka Eds.), pp. 191-95. Cambridge: Cambridge University Press

Torrence, R. 1989. Tools as optimal solutions in *Time, energy and stone tools* (R. Torrence Ed.), pp. 1-6. Cambridge: Cambridge University Press.

Trigger, B.G. 1978. *Time and Traditions*. Edinburg: Edinburg University Press.

Vinh, Bui 1994. The Mid-Holocene Transgression of the sea and cultural changes in the post-Hoabinh period of Vietnam. Paper presented in the 15th IPPA Congress, Chiang Mai, Thailand.

Vita-Finzi, C. 1969. *The Meditteranean Valleys*. Cambridge: Cambridge University Press.

Vita-Finzi, C. 1978. *Archaeological Site in their Setting*. London: Thames and Hudson Ltd.

Wagstaff, J. 1987. *Landscape and Culture*. London: Blackwell.

Walker, G.D. 1927. The Garo Manufacture of Bark Cloth, *Man* 5: 15-16.

Weinstock, J.A. 1984. Monoculture or Polyculture in a Swidden System, *Journal of Human Ecology* 12(4): 481.

White, J.P. 1969. Typologies for some prehistoric flaked stone artifacts of the Australian New Guinea Highlands, *Archaeology and Physical Anthropology in Oceania* 4(1): 18-46.

White, S.E. 1949. Processes of erosion on steep slopes of Oahu, Hawaii, *American Journal of Science* 247: 168-186.

Whittle, A. 1988. *Problems in Neolithic Archaeology*. Cambridge: Cambridge University Press.

Whyte, R.O. 1977. The Botanical Neolithic Revolution, *Journal of Human Ecology* 5(3): 209.

Worman, E.C. 1949. The Neolithic Problem in the Prehistory of India, *Journal of the Washington Academy of Sciences* 39(6): 181-200.

Yellen, J.E. 1977. *Ethnoarchaeology: Archaeological Approaches to the Present*. New York: Academic Press.

Yen, D.E. 1977. Hoabinhian Horticulture: The evidence and the questions from Northwest Thailand in *Sunda and Sahul: Prehistoric Studies in Southeast Asia, Melanesia and Australia* (J. Allen, J. Golson and R. Jones Eds.), pp. 567-599. New York: Academic Press.

Young, P.V. 1947. *Scientific Social Research*. New York: Prentice-Hall, Inc.

Zvelebil, M., S.W. Green and M.G. Macklin 1992. Archaeological Landscapes, Lithic Scatters and Human Behaviour in *Space, Time and Archaeological Landscape* (J. Rossignal and L. Wandsnider Eds.), pp. 193-225. New York & London: Plenum Press.

Zvelebil, M. (Ed.) 1986. *Hunters in Transition*. Cambridge: Cambridge University Press.

SOUTH ASIAN ARCHAEOLOGY SERIES

EDITED BY ALOK K. KANUNGO

SAA No 1. Kanungo, Alok Kumar 2004 *Glass Beads in Ancient India: An Ethnoarchaeological Approach* (*British Archaeological Reports, International Series* S1242) Oxford. ISBN 1 84171 364 3.

SAA No 2. Kanungo, Alok Kumar (Ed) 2005 *Gurudakshina: Facets of Indian Archaeology, Essays presented to Prof. V.N. Misra* (*British Archaeological Reports, International Series* S1433) Oxford. ISBN 1 84171 723 1.

SAA No 3. Swayam, S. 2006 *Invisible People: Pastoral life in Proto-Historic Gujurat* (*British Archaeological Reports, International Series* S1464) Oxford. ISBN 1 84171 732 0.

SAA No 4. Mushrif-Tripathy, Veena & Walimbe S.R. 2006 *Human Skeletal Remains from Chalcolithic Nevasa: Osteobiographic Analysis (British Archaeological Reports, International Series* S1476) Oxford. ISBN 1 84171 737 1.

SAA No 5. Jahan, Shahnaj Husne 2006 *Excavating Waves and Winds of (Ex)change: A Study of Maritime Trade in Early Bengal (British Archaeological Reports, International Series* S1533) Oxford. ISBN 1 84171 753 3.

SAA No 6. Pawankar, Seema J. 2007 *Man and Animal Relationship in Early Farming Communities of Western India, with Special Reference to Inamgaon (British Archaeological Reports, International Series* S1639) Oxford. ISBN 978 1 4073 0062 7.

SAA No 7. Sharma, Sukanya 2007 *Celts, Flakes and Bifaces – The Garo Hills Story (British Archaeological Reports, International Series* S1664) Oxford. ISBN 978 1 4073 0068 9.

www.ingramcontent.com/pod-product-compliance
Lightning Source LLC
Chambersburg PA
CBHW061301270326

41932CB00029B/3423